Road Trips,
Routes,
and Royals

A Baseball Fan's Journey
across the United States (and Canada)

John Brocato

Road Trips, Routes, and Royals
A Baseball Fan's Journey across the United States (and Canada)
All Rights Reserved.
Copyright © 2016 John Brocato
v3.0

Cover Photo © 2016 thinkstockphotos.com. All rights reserved - used with permission.

Outskirts Press, Inc.
http://www.outskirtspress.com

ISBN: 978-1-4787-7462-4

Outskirts Press and the "OP" logo are trademarks belonging to Outskirts Press, Inc.

PRINTED IN THE UNITED STATES OF AMERICA

outskirtspress
DENVER, COLORADO

Dedications

‖‖

I would like to dedicate this book to my three earliest travel companions—my parents Tony and Carol Brocato and my sister Laura Brocato. Dad has encouraged me to write about my travels for years. I am not an easy travel partner, but they usually indulged my frequent stop requests.

I would also like to dedicate this book in memory of the three grandparents that many of my first trips were to visit.

Leora J. Erickson ("Mommo"), 1906-2006
John C. Erickson ("Poppo"), 1905-1999
Mary P. Brocato ("Mamaw"), 1903-1991

To O—

I hope I can provide plenty of interesting places to see in our great country.

John Brocato
2/18/17

Table of Contents

Introduction

Traveling has always been an important part of my life. My mom is a native of St. Paul, Minnesota and my dad is a native of Helena, Arkansas. Visiting relatives, then, meant vacationing in opposite directions. My grandparents were unable to travel in the later years of their lives, so seeing them meant heading to their cities.

The Minnesota State Capitol with its distinctive gold Quadriga statue

The trips to Helena and St. Paul in the 1970s and 1980s offer a series of contrasts. When we went to Helena, Interstate 55 first took us to Memphis. We drove US Highway 61 through Mississippi, passing through Tunica many times before the city became a gambling hotbed. About 10 miles outside Helena, we traveled back west on US Highway 49 to re-enter Arkansas. The 370-mile drive to Helena was fast and easy, even back in the days of the national 55 mph speed limit.

The Delta Cultural Center in Helena, Arkansas

Driving to St. Paul, on the other hand, was a slow trip along mostly two-lane highways that Missouri, Iowa, and Minnesota have upgraded over the past 30 years. Interstate 380 through central Iowa opened in the 1980s, providing the fastest 72 miles of the 500+ mile trip. The drive was long and exhausting when completed in one day. However, those trips gave me new appreciation for the small towns of the Midwest.

My young mind started to notice some of the peculiarities of the trips. One common thread of St. Paul, Helena, and my hometown outside St. Louis was that my parents, sister, and I all grew up near the Mississippi River. My childhood was spent in the waning days of Missouri's "blue laws", so it was not uncommon for Missourians to line up on the old bridge into Alton to visit the mall on Sunday afternoon. At an early age, I learned that the Mississippi River was the divide between Missouri and Illinois, between Arkansas and Tennessee, and between Arkansas and Mississippi. However, I could not grasp that you could cross the Mississippi River in Minnesota without changing states!

The drive to Helena had two aspects that seemed quirky to the young me. I remember thinking it strange that our preferred route entered Arkansas, but then left the state at Memphis, before finishing in Arkansas. Once my math skills started developing, I observed that most of the drive was spent in my native Missouri.

As my sister and I grew older, we branched off into other destinations besides St. Paul and Helena. In 1984 we expanded the Helena trip to include Nashville and the Grand Ole Opry and a visit to the World's Fair in New Orleans. The next summer's trip to St. Paul included my first venture into Canada as we spent four nights in Winnipeg. We traveled to Milwaukee in 1988 and attended the annual Circus Parade, along with a baseball game at the long-gone County Stadium. In the summer of 1990 we took a family vacation to Walt Disney World, changing from our usual motels to stay at the Peabody Orlando. Some of our destinations were less common, such as Lincoln, Nebraska, Sioux Falls, South Dakota, and Thunder Bay, Ontario.

Once I began to earn a reliable paycheck, I started planning my own vacations. Whether you call it fortune or misfortune to be a Kansas City Royals fan living near St. Louis, I realized that if I planned my own trips, I could see the Royals play more often while also exploring more of the United States (and occasionally, Canada). In July 2005 I took a brief four-day trip to Cleveland, the first time I had traveled solo to an unfamiliar city. The next year I traveled to Pittsburgh and Cincinnati and my summer trip became an annual event that I started thinking about when Major League Baseball issued the following season's schedule each September.

Even though my grandparents have been gone for years, my travels are shaped by the childhood trips to St. Paul and Helena. My trips typically include time on the interstates, sometimes with 80 mph speed limits, but I try to take part of the trip on the two-lane roads through small towns. I have lost track of how many places I have crossed the Mississippi and Missouri Rivers. Bus rides in St. Paul with my grandparents often passed the Minnesota State Capitol, and now I find myself visiting the capitol buildings as I add new states. St. Paul and its twin Minneapolis each had downtown department stores and to this day, I still enjoy this dying breed more than their suburban counterparts.

Many travel guides are written each year covering different topics like Orlando theme parks, the attractions of Texas, Europe on a budget, and so on. There are comprehensive directories to major- and minor-league ballparks. I am not trying to copy these efforts. I am writing this book to share my passion for travel. I love this country's variety from the large cities to the small towns, from the well-known landmarks to the frivolous. I've often said that it's easier for me to travel solo because I stop on the spur of the moment if I see the interesting and unexpected.

Another disclaimer is that until I make my first trips to Alaska, Hawaii, or overseas, my travels are by car. It goes without saying that when traveling from the Midwest to Seattle, flying is faster. Although we flew to Minnesota each Christmas when I was a child, I prefer driving to my destination. You see much more along the way and there is always the possibility of a surprise, such as Shoshone Falls in Idaho or the Museum of the Rockies in Montana. Many of the fun places to visit are nowhere near an international airport.

Enjoy this sampling of my vacation experiences. Happy traveling!

John Brocato

CHAPTER 1

Getting Started

||||||||||||||||||||||||||||||||||||||||||||||||||||||||||||||||||||||||||||||||||||||||||||||||||||||||||||||||||||||||||||||||||||||||||||||||||||||||||||||

The September day that Major League Baseball issues its schedule for the following season is much like Christmas for me. As a teacher, I am limited to planning major trips in June and July, so I first look to see if the Kansas City Royals are playing in any unfamiliar cities. For instance, when the 2015 schedule was released, I noticed the Royals had a series from June 22-24 in Seattle. Having never traveled west of Denver and Colorado Springs, I immediately decided that I wanted to plan a trip to the Pacific Northwest.

Two landmarks immediately came to mind when thinking about Seattle—the Space Needle and Pike Place Market. I knew both sites would be required on my first visit to Seattle. As my trip drew closer, I used the Tourbook from the American Automobile Association to learn about other attractions. I also talked with a long-time friend from college who had vacationed in Seattle several years prior.

Since I would be traveling by car from Missouri to Washington, I then set out to figure what other cities and attractions would be along the way. Some trips allow me to discover more than one new ballpark, but there are no other major-league teams even close to Seattle. The Royals have their Rookie League affiliate in Idaho Falls and the schedule allowed me to attend their season opener. Their Triple-A club is in Omaha, which I would pass through on the way home. I also scheduled a game of the Mariners Triple-A team in Tacoma and made a last-minute decision to attend a Class-A game in Boise. In addition, I was able to see the Royals play at Kauffman Stadium on the last night of my trip.

This trip included three states I had never visited—Montana, Idaho, and Washington. The bus rides with my grandparents in St. Paul interested me in capitols, so each time I visit new states, I plan the capitol buildings. Of the 41 states I have visited, the only two capitol buildings I have not toured belong to Alabama and Maryland, the latter having been closed for HVAC renovations during my 2008 trip. Although this meant taking a far-from-direct route, I intentionally routed my trip through Helena, Montana and Boise, Idaho with a side trip to Olympia, Washington.

A perk of being the son of a Minnesota native is that my mom is familiar with many of the major Canadian cities. She introduced my sister and me to Canada before we were in junior high with a family trip to Winnipeg. I acquired a passport in 2012 to see the Royals play in Toronto, a trip that also included stops in Montreal and Ottawa. Two years later I incorporated two nights in Quebec City as part of a New England tour. I noticed that Seattle is close to both Vancouver and Victoria and first hoped to include both cities. However, after sitting down with the calendar, I soon realized that my schedule permitted only one city. I chose Vancouver since the ferry trip to Victoria would have eaten up a considerable amount of sightseeing time.

Narrowing down the natural attractions required studying the map. Some of my friends have raved about Glacier National Park, but I decided it was too far out of the way when I planned to see the Royals minor-league affiliate play in Idaho Falls. Since I had not traveled to the western states, I decided that reaching the Pacific Ocean would be an important goal and given that I was already headed to Olympia, Washington, I continued out to Ocean Shores. The second place I wanted to visit was Old Faithful, so I figured I would spend part of a travel day at Yellowstone National Park. More on this later, but I greatly underestimated the size and popularity of Yellowstone. The third natural attraction on the original itinerary was the Badlands in South Dakota. Given the number of miles I was traveling, I was grateful that I had seen Mount Rushmore, the Crazy Horse Memorial, and Devils Tower on my 2011 trip.

As a lifelong United Methodist, I have visited a number of churches on my vacations. Since I found a Point Break hotel in Boise, I decided that spending a second night in Boise would be restful after several long drives, and I would attend First United Methodist Church, nick-named the Cathedral of the Rockies. The church has many stained-glass windows, including incorporating an Idaho potato into one of the scenes, and a large pipe organ. The next week I attended Garden Street United Methodist Church in Bellingham, Washington, with its 10:30 service allowing me enough time to pass through customs coming south from British Columbia. When I identified myself as a visitor from Missouri, the minister told me that he attended seminary at Saint Paul School of Theology in Kansas City.

One of my favorite parts of planning travel is identifying the routes. Not only am I a capitol and ballpark collector, but I also count the counties. Several years ago I discovered a website, www.mob-rule.com/home, where users can keep track of the counties they have visited, along with Louisiana's parishes and independent cities like St. Louis and Baltimore. I try to add new counties in familiar states and it is also fun to see how many counties I visit in the new states. Although much of the trip would require interstate travel, I was able to plan some two-lane meandering through Iowa, Nebraska, Wyoming, and Idaho.

A similar process has guided me through many other trips through the years. I roll ideas through my mind for months and make the final plans in the weeks leading to departure. Many times I discover unex-pected sites along the way as I will share in the following chapters.

CHAPTER 2

Stretching My Travel Dollar

I have found ways to travel better than I could otherwise afford. Having a fuel-efficient car is most important, especially when traveling past signs that read "NEXT SERVICES 66 MILES". What really aids my travel plans, though, is reward programs.

My car of choice is a 2010 Toyota Corolla, on which I have put 216,000 miles in the first six years. This car replaced a 2002 Corolla, which had 236,000 miles in eight years. Both cars were manufactured in the United States. There are a number of fuel-efficient cars you can choose from, but having a car that averages more than 30 miles per gallon is essential.

Hotel reward programs allow travelers to earn free nights and each year I typically use about $1000 worth of free lodging. Nearly every major lodging chain has a rewards program. I belong to three hotel programs: IHG Rewards Club (formerly Priority Club), Hilton HHonors, and Red Roof Redicard. The key to maximizing my rewards is to pay for nights in less expensive markets and use free nights in pricier cities. There is not necessarily a pattern as to where hotels are more expensive and rates can often be surprising. For instance—a free Holiday Inn Express night in Gillette, Wyoming might be more valuable than a free Holiday Inn Express night in Brooklyn, New York.

My most-commonly used program is the IHG Rewards Club. IHG hotels include Holiday Inn, Holiday Inn Express, Candlewood Suites,

Staybridge Suites, and other high-end and boutique properties. There are several reasons why this is my hotel program of first choice. Many free nights require only 10,000-20,000 points and "Point Break" specials offer rooms for only 5000 points per night. Members can earn Elite status rapidly: Gold with 10,000 qualifying points or 10 nights per year, Platinum with 40,000 qualifying points or 40 nights, and Spire with 75,000 qualifying points or 75 nights. Perks with higher levels include bonus points and sometimes individual hotels offer rewards such as snack bags or free breakfast.

Reward nights have allowed me to stay free at hotels I might not have otherwise afforded. For instance, in the summer of 2012, I stayed four nights at a Holiday Inn in downtown Toronto where the only cost was $15/night for parking. The hotel was convenient to Toronto's subway system and the only time I moved my car during the stay was to visit Niagara Falls. The next year I stayed free at a Holiday Inn Express in Cooperstown, several miles from the National Baseball Hall of Fame. Among the metro areas where I have used free hotel stays are Brooklyn, Baltimore, St. Petersburg, Vancouver, Montreal, Houston, and the Black Hills region around Rapid City.

Of the hotels in the Hilton HHonors program, I am most familiar with Hampton Inn. I have not been a member of this program for as long as IHG Rewards, so I have only redeemed one free night in a Chicago suburb. Most hotels require a minimum of 20,000 points for a free stay, but many of the hotels in the program are higher-end chains such as Hilton. Members can also earn HHonors points through shopping in their Shop-to-Earn Mall.

Both IHG Rewards and Hilton HHonors points can be earned through the Rewards Network Dining Club program. Each year I earn thousands of points dining at participating restaurants. Many of the St. Louis area restaurants in the program such as Kirkwood Station, Pickles Deli, and Highway 61 Roadhouse are among my favorites and the latter was even spotlighted by Guy Fieri on a 2012 episode of *Diners, Drive-Ins, and Dives*. Coincidentally I discovered Guy Fieri's American Kitchen & Bar near Times Square through the Rewards

Network dining program. Many of the restaurants in the program display their menus on the website, so it is easy to find a spot suitable to one's taste and price range. This is an easy way to learn about restaurants in unfamiliar cities and take a break from national chains while earning points toward free hotel stays.

Another way to earn IHG Rewards and Hilton HHonors points is by completing surveys in the E-Rewards program. Surveys are sent to my e-mail box on a regular basis and completed surveys earn anywhere from $1.50 to $12 and once the account has a high enough balance, the credit can be converted to hotel points. I usually earn about 16,000-20,000 IHG points per year through E-Rewards and the best part is that they do not cost me a cent.

In recent years gas stations have begun offering reward programs. I am a member of Fuel Rewards, which provides a minimum 3 cent per gallon savings at participating Shell stations. The Fuel Rewards website offers online shopping and other ways to knock down the price of gasoline. Hy-Vee, a grocery store found in the Midwest and Great Plains, has a card that may be linked to Fuel Rewards cards and certain purchases will earn savings at either Shell or the Hy-Vee gas stations. The Kroger Plus cards also earn points for savings at their gas stations or at Shell stations located near Kroger stores. Chains in the Kroger family include Harris-Teeter, King Soopers, and Fred Meyer, among others.

Plenti is one of the newest reward programs. Gasoline purchases at Exxon or Mobil earn 1 point per gallon and convenience-store purchases earn 2 points per dollar. Other participating retailers include Macy's and Rite-Aid. With at least 200 points, members can save money at the participating stores. Plenti also has an online marketplace.

Although not directly connected to travel, two of the longer-running online rewards programs are MyPoints and Memolink. MyPoints offers points for watching videos, performing searches, clicking on links in e-mails, playing online games, completing surveys, and shopping. Points may be exchanged for gift cards to department stores, restaurants, discount stores, gas stations, and other places. Memolink offers points by shopping online, clicking on links in e-mails, completing surveys, and answering trivia questions. Memolink points may be exchanged for cash, e-gift cards, and magazine subscriptions.

Two final programs worth mentioning are Coca-Cola's My Coke Rewards and Walgreens Balance Rewards. Entering codes found on caps and in larger packages of the many Coca-Cola brands earn points that can be redeemed for a number of items. Periodically, points may be exchanged for hotel-chain points, but these prizes are infrequent. Getting items for free that I would have purchased anyway frees up money for travel. I have redeemed Walgreens Balance Rewards points when printing my vacation photos.

Although completing surveys and clicking on e-mail links takes time, I have found that the time spent with these programs allows me to increase my travel budget. Best of all, there is no fee to join any of these programs!

CHAPTER 3

A Few of My Favorite Things

Following completion of Missouri's annual standardized tests, several years ago my colleagues and I aired *The Sound of Music* for the entire seventh grade. The musical includes many catchy songs that last in everybody's heads all day. Each of us could write songs about our favorite things, though perhaps without using the lyrics "schnitzel with noodles". Some of my favorite aspects of travel were shaped in childhood.

Capitol buildings are often among the most magnificent buildings in each state. Although I rode the St. Paul bus past the Minnesota State Capitol many times growing up, I did not actually enter the building until 2000, at a time when the capitol was receiving many tourists due to the national attention provided by their then-governor, former pro wrestler Jesse Ventura. Since then, I have toured 37 other capitol buildings from Olympia, Washington to Tallahassee, Florida.

Whether a classic dome like many states or a skyscraper like North Dakota, Nebraska, Florida, or Louisiana, each capitol building tells the story of its state. The murals and the statues depict the people who shaped the state. Often the murals portray the state values such as agriculture, justice, or education. Some tour guides are great narrators. For instance, when I toured the Texas State Capitol in 2009, the guide asked if anybody knew the name of the statue on top of the rotunda (the Goddess of Liberty). I do not recall anyone in our tour answering the question correctly and the tour guide said he had received answers ranging from Willie Nelson to Jesus, neither of which would have surprised me in Texas. My Arkansas visit passed through the state treasurer's office where I was allowed to hold $240,000 in cash; this was one tour I wish provided free samples! Massachusetts has a Sacred Cod hanging in its House chamber.

The capital cities have great variety. Montpelier is a small town with the capitol building blending into the downtown area, much like a county courthouse. Denver, Austin, and Atlanta are large cities with numerous other tourist attractions. The approach to the Kentucky Capitol is scenic with the state house located on the Kentucky River. Missouri and West Virginia also have capitol buildings located along rivers. The interior of the Pennsylvania State Capitol is especially beautiful. The skyscraper capitols offer observation decks.

When passing through small-town America, I often drive into the downtown of the county seat. Many counties have impressive courthouse buildings, many of which are located on town squares. One of my favorite courthouses is the Davis County Courthouse in Bloomfield, Iowa.

Small-town Midwest has many elegant courthouses,
often set up in the center of town squares such as
the Davis County Courthouse in Bloomfield, Iowa.

My childhood Minnesota experiences included trips to downtown department stores, many of which have been closing in recent years. Downtown St. Paul is left without a large retailer after once having Dayton's (later Marshall Field's, then Macy's) and Donaldson's (later Carson Pirie Scott). Minneapolis had Dayton's, Donaldson's, Powers, and Saks Fifth Avenue; the former Dayton's flagship continues today as Macy's with a statue of Mary Tyler Moore tossing her hat in the air outside the store. Many of today's surviving downtown stores became Macy's in 2006.

Sadly, Macy's has closed two of my favorite downtown locations in recent years. One of my favorite treats on a Friday day off was to visit the St. Louis flagship and dine at the buffet in the St. Louis Room on the sixth floor. The buffet had excellent fried cod, macaroni and cheese, and the best banana pudding. The honeydew and cantaloupe were always of the highest quality. Each Christmas the windows were decorated, with a large model railroad set up at one corner. Unfortunately, the store was downsized in 2011, ultimately leading to its closure two years later.

The other flagship Macy's I especially miss was in downtown Pittsburgh. The main interstates bypass the heart of Pittsburgh, but when I traveled east, I would drive out of the way to eat at the Tic Toc Restaurant. The gold clock on the corner, known as the Kaufmann's Clock for the original department store tenant was a popular meeting spot in Pittsburgh. The Tic Toc Restaurant had great desserts and in the unlikely chance I was still hungry, I could visit the Arcade Bakery in the mezzanine.

Philadelphia's downtown Macy's is known for the Wanamaker Organ, a six-manual model built for the 1904 World's Fair in St. Louis. Several years later John Wanamaker purchased the organ for his Philadelphia store. Two concerts are performed each day from Monday through Saturday and visitors can ride a city bus from the Independence Hall area to the store.

My favorite emporium is Macy's on State Street in the Chicago Loop. The former Marshall Field's has many distinctive architectural features including a clock on the corner of State and Washington, a stained-glass ceiling, fountains, and an eight-story atrium. Customers have many dining options including the elegant Walnut Room, the Frango Café, and lower-level food court. One of the most flavorful sandwiches I have eaten was turkey on grilled cinnamon bread in the Frango Café. In 2003 I attended the Royals season opener in Chicago and had the chance to visit the annual flower show in the ninth-floor event center. The store has an extensive variety of Frango chocolates, some in distinctive Chicago boxes. The other Macy's known for Frango mints is in downtown Seattle, with the chocolates sold in hexagon-shaped packages.

Every president from Herbert Hoover through George W. Bush has a presidential library. I developed an interest in Harry Truman at an early age when I realized that not only were we both Missouri natives, but we shared the same birthday. The first presidential library I visited was the Truman Library in Independence. Each museum tells the story of the president's life and time in office. The older libraries like Hoover, Truman, and Eisenhower are smaller galleries while the more recent presidents have built huge shrines. As with capitol buildings, presidential libraries can be found in small towns like West Branch, Iowa (Hoover) or large cities like Boston (Kennedy) and Atlanta (Carter).

When traveling solo, I listen to country music, either on CD or radio. Every country music fan needs to attend a show at the Grand Ole Opry in Nashville. Each week the live radio show includes a variety from Hall of Famers Bill Anderson and Jean Shepard to newer singers like Carrie Underwood and Scotty McCreery. Most shows include bluegrass and gospel music. Dad and I attended the 2011 show when Bill Anderson celebrated his 50th anniversary at the Opry. The show opened with the late legend Little Jimmy Dickens telling jokes about his old age, such as the time he switched his hearing aid with a suppository. Another highlight of the evening was Ronnie Milsap performing his hit *Smoky Mountain Rain*. One of my memories of my family's 1984 Nashville trip was when the late Hall of Famer Skeeter Davis sang *The End of the World*.

Each week is a special occasion at the Grand Ole Opry,
a radio program that has run for more than 90 years.

Nashville is home to the Country Music Hall of Fame and Museum. The museum tells a complete history of the genre and at the end, guests enter a rotunda with the plaques of all the inductees arranged like notes on a musical staff. During my 2011 visit, the special exhibit was on the Williams family and one of my favorite pieces of memorabilia was a 1948 Grand Ole Opry program showing Little Jimmy Dickens on the same bill as Hank Williams Sr. Since we had seen Dickens the night before, we had new appreciation for his longevity.

Tourists wishing to expand their country-music library need to visit the Ernest Tubb Record Shop downtown. The store has an extensive selection of compact discs and the danger of visiting the store is that I can easily spend $200 on one trip. What makes this shop stand out is the selection of recordings from decades ago, not just new releases. In addition to two Nashville stores, there is a third shop in Pigeon Forge, Tennessee.

Two radio stations stand out for providing country music across a wide listening area. Country music radio starts with WSM 650 out of Nashville, the flagship station of the Grand Ole Opry. At night, WSM can be heard over much of the eastern United States. The evening Eddie Stubbs Show is hosted by a country-music expert who plays many long-forgotten recordings on his show.

Another notable country station is based in an unexpected city— Jamestown, North Dakota. KSJB 600 has such a powerful signal that even in daytime, I picked up the station as far west as Devils Tower in Wyoming. The station provides news from both North and South Dakota, weather reports extending to Winnipeg and western Minnesota, and many familiar country songs. The one danger of listening to the station in Wyoming and the western Dakotas is remembering that when the disc jockey gives the time, Jamestown is in the Central Time Zone.

When possible, if a country song has a geographic reference, I like to play that song when I travel through the mentioned city or state. My first timing of a song was to listen to Billy Walker's *Cross the Brazos at Waco* while driving to a Texas barbecue restaurant. The next week I was on Galveston Island, the logical place to listen to Glen Campbell sing *Galveston*. Willie Nelson's *City of New Orleans* was perfect listening in the Crescent City. John Denver's *Rocky Mountain High* provided a backdrop in Colorado and *Take Me Home, Country Roads* was ideal for West Virginia. As I approached the Dwight Eisenhower Presidential Museum in 2011, I listened to George Hamilton IV sing *Abilene*. Connie Smith sang *Cincinnati, Ohio* and Lefty Frizzell *Saginaw, Michigan* while I drove through the respective Midwestern cities.

Glen Campbell embarked on a farewell tour in 2011, shortly after his diagnosis with Alzheimer's disease. My parents and I attended his concert at Lindenwood University in St. Charles, Missouri. When he performed *Galveston*, I closed my eyes and pictured Seawall

Boulevard and the waves of the Gulf of Mexico in the scenic Texas community.

While Julie Andrews may never sing about country music or presidential libraries, my favorite things have been an important part of my travels, sometimes as much so as the baseball stadiums. I hope to eventually visit all the state capitol buildings and presidential libraries.

CHAPTER 4

Food, Glorious Food

Food tourism takes different forms. Makers of many established grocery products have set up visitor centers and offer factory tours. These factory tours often include samples. A second variety of food tourism is the discovery of restaurants in different cities, or regional chains not found in my community.

Ben & Jerry's Ice Cream put Waterbury, Vermont on the map.

Most of my traveling takes place during the hot summer months and an ice cream factory is always a welcome site. When planning my 2012 trip through the Canadian cities of Toronto, Ottawa, and Montreal, I decided to spend a weekend in Vermont with the Ben & Jerry's Ice Cream Factory in Vermont as a top priority. The tour includes a video of the company history, overview of the factory, and a free sample at the end. Following my tour, I walked off the ice cream by exploring a graveyard of discontinued Ben & Jerry's flavors.

In 2007 Dad and I were exploring western Iowa and discovered LeMars, known as the Ice Cream Capital of the World. Since we were in LeMars, Blue Bunny has restored a downtown building for its showcase parlor. Photos and exhibits were moved into their new location.

One of my favorite regional chains is Braum's, based in Oklahoma City with locations in the Southern Plains and Ozark regions. While Braum's has a typical fast-food menu, their specialty is ice cream. A large number of ice cream flavors are available each day, any of which can be made into shakes or malts. What distinguishes Braum's from a common fast-food chain is that each location includes a small grocery store with produce, meat, and Braum's brands of cereal, baked goods, and frozen meals. Any trip to southwest Missouri or Oklahoma always has to include at least one visit to Braum's.

Located several minutes north of Ben & Jerry's, not as well-known, but just as worthwhile is the Cold Hollow Cider Mill. Visitors may take self-guided tours of the cider-making process and sample the finished product. The cider doughnuts are an absolute must. Vermont maple syrup is featured predominantly in the gift shop, but a number of other items including jams and jellies, mustard, and relish are sold, as well. One danger of visiting Vermont is developing a taste for genuine maple syrup!

My 2010 trip to Atlanta had a long list of places to see—three Royals games at Turner Field, the Georgia State Capitol, the Jimmy Carter Presidential Library, and the Martin Luther King Jr. National Historic Site. One additional attraction caught my eye—the World of Coca-Cola. The World of Coca-Cola is one of the most comprehensive food museums with a 4-D theater, video room with a continuous loop of Coke commercials through the years, and a gallery of Coca-Cola art. The final area is a tasting room with dozens of Coca-Cola products throughout the world and samples are unlimited. If you decide to taste the Beverly soda, just remember you have been warned! Participants in the My Coke Rewards program often have the opportunity to redeem their points for free admission to World of Coca-Cola.

As I was driving across Pennsylvania in the summer of 2008, I escaped the turnpike and visited the town of Hershey. The main thoroughfare through town is called Chocolate Avenue and the city's streetlights are shaped like Hershey's kisses. Visitors get to know Milton Hershey at the Museum on Chocolate Avenue. I also recommend visiting the attractions of Hershey Chocolate World. When traveling through central Pennsylvania, I also took the guided tour of the Gettysburg National Military Park and in Harrisburg visited one of the most beautiful state capitol buildings.

Chelsea, Michigan is home to the Jiffy Mix factory and tours of the plant are given on weekdays. Samples included baked Jiffy goods and two boxes of mix. The Jiffy Mix factory is located off Interstate 94 about 20 miles west of Ann Arbor.

After my Jiffy Mix tour, I planned to head northeast through the tiny Michigan town of Hell. Many people mail postcards from Hell and there is a small dining area called Hell's Kitchen. The town is located off the main highways, but with its name I was embarrassed to ask for directions. I started to ask, "There is a town northeast of here that I am trying to find" and was quickly interrupted, "You mean, Hell, Michigan?" I said that was the town and the worker was helpful in telling me how to go to Hell. Ironically, the temperature in Hell that morning was 67°, which meant that on my two-week trip, the coolest weather I encountered was in Hell! Some year I would like to drive to Michigan in winter and see if Hell has frozen over.

Hell, the town in Michigan, even has its own post office.

For the opportunity to see candy canes in the middle of summer, I visited the town of Bryan in northwest Ohio. The Spangler Candy Factory offers tours on the Dum-Dum Trolley, a smart way to spend a July afternoon. Visitors can taste proposed flavors of Dum-Dums before they are offered for sale. Spangler also makes Saf-T-Pops and is one of the largest manufacturers of candy canes. When I toured the plant in July 2013, palettes of candy cane boxes awaited shipment later in the year.

When traveling through Ohio and the eastern states, one of my favorite chain restaurants is Friendly's. Like Braum's in the Great Plains, Friendly's specializes in ice cream. Their milkshakes, called Fribbles, are delicious. Unlike Braum's, Friendly's is a sit-down restaurant with sandwiches, salads, soups, and entrees. I have eaten in a number of locations from New Hampshire to Florida and every meal was delicious.

I had a busy day traveling the Interstate 95 corridor between Boston and New York City in 2014. Before leaving Boston, I walked around the Harvard campus. My route through Rhode Island purposely included all five of the state's counties. Connecticut offered two junk-food memories. I stopped at the state's welcome center and picked up a brochure of Connecticut's Sundae Drives, a directory of the ice cream parlors in the state. Once I had enjoyed my cone, I continued toward New York City and stopped at the PEZ Visitor Center in Orange. The self-guided tour shows videos of the dispenser design and candy-making processes. The highlight is a series of display racks of thousands of different PEZ dispensers through the years, covering sports and pop culture, in addition to international PEZ products. Visitors may also win a PEZ dispenser by completing a scavenger hunt.

Carlo's Bake Shop is located minutes from New York City in Hoboken, New Jersey and is the bakery featured in the television show *Cake Boss*. The cupcakes and cookies are worth the wait. Customers can buy merchandise autographed by Buddy Valastro. I learned to arrive before 9 am when there is almost no line and no charge to park. My first trip to the bakery was in mid-afternoon when parking cost $15 and the wait to enter the store was nearly an hour.

A South Dakota bucket list needs to include Mount Rushmore, the Crazy Horse Monument, Wall Drug, and the Corn Palace. The Corn Palace is covered each year with artwork comprised of corn kernels. Each year the Mitchell landmark selects a different theme—for instance, when I visited in 2009, the theme was America's Destinations. Admission is free.

Minutes after my windshield's unfortunate encounter with a rock, I found the Idaho Potato Museum in Blackfoot. The World's Largest Pringle is on display in the former railroad depot. Another showcase includes a collection of Mr. Potato Head toys. Vintage potato farming equipment takes up a large segment of the museum. The museum also gives visitors from outside Idaho a free bag of mashed potato mix through their "free taters for out-of-staters" promotion. Later in the day I took the Idaho Falls Chukars fan's advice and dined on French fries as part of a meal in Boise. The next day, also in Boise, I had one of my favorite meals of the 2015 western trip—fish and chips at McGrath's Fish House.

As a Royals fan, I have plenty of opportunities to eat Kansas City barbecue. Gates is one of the best-known restaurants with several locations in the area. One of my favorites is Winslow's, located at the River Market downtown. Jack Stack has multiple locations and the Famous Dave's chain also sells high-quality barbecue. While in Kansas City, I recommend the burnt ends sandwich.

One benefit of being a Royals fan living in the St. Louis area is stopping at Shakespeare's Pizza in Columbia on the way home from games. Shakespeare's was voted Best College Town Hangout by *Good Morning America* in 2010. Their pizza is well-known across the Show-Me State. The restrooms at Shakespeare's have one of my favorite reminders, "Of course, employees must wash their hands—and you should, too!"

Having traveled to Dad's Arkansas hometown numerous times, I have seen countless billboards for Lambert's Café in Sikeston, Missouri. A huge appetite is required for their large portions of southern cuisine. Lambert's is known nationally for "throwed" rolls—the servers throw large dinner rolls at the customers. I wait to eat the roll after a "pass around" of sorghum molasses; servers also bring around free helpings of okra, macaroni with tomato, and other side items. I recommend buying a "hubcap" cinnamon roll to take home. Lambert's also has locations in Ozark, Missouri and Foley, Alabama.

In Chapter 2 I mentioned discovering restaurants through the Rewards Network Dining Program with one of my finds being Guy Fieri's American Kitchen & Bar on West 44th Street in Manhattan. Compared to many restaurants in the Big Apple, Guy Fieri's is relatively affordable and I recommend the sourdough pretzel-encrusted chicken tenders.

When taking the Gray Line tour of New York City in 2013, the guide encouraged us to stop at Magnolia Bakery for banana pudding.

The bakery was seen in the television show *Sex and the City* and in the movie *The Devil Wears Prada*. Magnolia Bakery has several locations in New York, as well as one on Chicago's State Street and another in Los Angeles. The banana pudding is my favorite, but their cupcakes are delicious, as well. Although I have enjoyed great food in New York City, I like to tell people that I never did see the factory that makes salsa not under the Pace brand.

Although sometimes I will stop at the familiar national and international chains, I intentionally try to find at least one restaurant not found at home on each day of travel. The visitor centers of the familiar food products are fun and I bring home edible souvenirs from the gift shops.

CHAPTER 5

Tales of the Unexpected

One of the joys of traveling is the surprise discovery. Whenever I visit a city for the first time, I enter with a solid idea of the major attractions. Capitol buildings, stadiums, and downtown department stores are well-known and easy to find. I use AAA books and the IHG Rewards Network dining program to research restaurants. Sometimes, though, the best discoveries come from a green sign on the interstate, a tear-off map at the hotel, or a chat with other baseball fans. None of the activities in this chapter were included in my original travel plans, but looking back, I am glad that I learned about each of these locations and events.

Austin, Texas was a natural inclusion on my 2009 trip to see the Royals play in Houston for two reasons—the state capitol and the Lyndon B. Johnson Presidential Museum. I arrived in Austin in mid-afternoon and toured the capitol, saving the Johnson Museum for the next morning. While in Austin, I also planned dinner at the Furr's cafeteria, remembering their fried chicken fondly from when the chain had Missouri locations. I did not know much else about Austin, other than it was a fast-growing Sunbelt city along Interstate 35.

The movement to "Keep Austin Weird" caught my attention. I learned about the Congress Avenue Bridge, known as the "Bat Bridge" for the colony of bats that reside underneath. Each evening just before dusk the bats emerge. I thought this might be a small curiosity, drawing a few people each evening. Much to my surprise, I had to park my then-new car several blocks away from the bridge. Dancers and singers entertained the crowds waiting for the bats and wise entrepreneurs hawked water and other cold beverages. The sight of thousands of small bats escaping the bottom of the bridge and flying over Lady Bird Lake and city was not something I expected in an urban center.

After spending a week in Texas, I drove to Louisiana to visit the state capitol in Baton Rouge and attend my first Triple-A baseball game in New Orleans. When I checked into my hotel in New Orleans, I called Dad and asked him what I should do there since he attended college in the Crescent City. He sent me to two places, one for lunch and the other for dessert. The first was Camellia Grill, which would later finish as the runner-up to Shakespeare's Pizza in the *Good Morning America* contest for best college-town hangout. My last stop in New Orleans was at Angelo Brocato Ice Cream. I enjoyed the ice cream and brought home a bag of biscotti; my only disagreement was how to pronounce our shared last name. Unlike my family, they do not pronounce Brocato with three long vowels.

Among the many great ice cream parlors is this one in New Orleans
with the author's last name on the store

The next summer I traveled to watch the Royals play an inter-league series in Atlanta, followed by a Rays/Padres game at Tropicana Field in St. Petersburg. After the Braves swept the Royals, I spent much of my drive to Valdosta steaming about the poor baseball I had watched that weekend. When I crossed into Florida the next morning, I entered the Sunshine State for the first time since my family's 1990 trip to Disney World. Florida has built a tourist industry of its beaches and theme parks, but I enjoyed two lesser-known activities.

Whenever I visit a different region, I try to experience an activity unique to the area. The year before I was disappointed by having to cancel an alligator-farm tour in Louisiana due to threatening weather—a decision proven wise almost immediately after leaving Natchitoches. I heard about a dolphin cruise in Tampa Bay that guaranteed dolphin sightings or visitors could take a second cruise free. The two-hour cruise ventured out into the bay and the guide pointed out St. Petersburg landmarks and the Al Lang Field spring-training venue. However, we were not having any luck finding dolphins. Luckily, the captain knew how to attract the dolphins' attention and during the last part of the cruise, we saw a number of dolphins. Besides the animals' beauty, I enjoyed riding out onto a large body of water.

Florida is typically a state not associated with U. S. presidents, which is why I was surprised to find the Presidents Hall of Fame in Clermont, between Tampa and Orlando. The museum covers all the presidents from George Washington through Barack Obama with an emphasis on items such as White House china and ornaments. Seat H-7 from the Ford Theater where Abraham Lincoln was assassinated is displayed. A photograph of five presidents taken during the George H. W. Bush administration caught my eye, especially since I was born during a brief period in which there were no living ex-presidents. People who enjoy learning about the presidents should spend time at the Presidents Hall of Fame.

I was driving to Omaha in June 2014, eagerly anticipating two activities that day—buying Dutch apple bread at Jaarsma Bakery in Pella, Iowa and watching the Royals Triple-A affiliate play that evening. Usually I approach Pella from the north, so I was not familiar with US Highway 34 between Mt. Pleasant and Ottumwa. I expected to drive non-stop between Mt. Pleasant and Pella until a highway sign advertised the American Gothic Home in Eldon. Visitors learn about Grant Wood and can have their picture taken in front of the house made famous in his painting *American Gothic*. I wore the coat and held a pitchfork for my photo, but maintaining the farmer's solemn look without breaking into laughter was a challenge.

The author stands in front of the American Gothic Home in Eldon, Iowa. It was very hard to maintain the dour pose without breaking up in laughter.

Later that summer I stopped in Chicago on my way home from New York. Naturally I planned a trip to the Art Institute so I could see the original *American Gothic* painting. Georges Seurat's *A Sunday Afternoon on the Island of La Grande Jatte* grabbed my attention because the painting was featured in a geometry book I used as a first-year teacher.

Microsoft co-founder Paul Allen opened the Living Computer Museum, one of Seattle's newer attractions. The museum displays decades of working computers, in some cases, guests can even try some of the earlier models, including a keypunch machine. Visitors may challenge each other to the early video game Pong. Early Atari games reminded me just how primitive the graphics were in the video games I played growing up in the 1980s. (That said, I would still rather opt for Ms. Pac-Man or pinball over any present-day video game!) While driving to the museum from Interstate 5, I passed the world headquarters for Starbucks.

While chatting with residents of the Seattle area during the Royals 2015 series at Safeco Field, I mentioned that once the Royals left town, I would be driving to Vancouver. Several people suggested that I drive the Sea to Sky Highway, Route 99, between Vancouver and Whistler. Stops along the road provide breathtaking views of Howe Sound and the Coast Mountains. Distance signs spell out the city names in both English and the Squamish language.

Whistler hosted Nordic skiing, bobsledding, and luge events during the 2010 Winter Olympics. The town boasts a small village consisting of tourist shops, restaurants, hotels, and services. I lunched on a panini sandwich at a bakery/café called Hot Buns, but the best part was apple-pie flavored ice cream at Cows Creamery. Over the last few years I have discovered many new ice cream flavors, but this was my first involving apple. The Squamish Lil'wat Cultural Centre tells the history and customs of the people indigenous to southwestern British Columbia and visitors learn how to make cedar rope.

Most cities and regions have more activities than I could reasonably fit into a single vacation. I return from each vacation with ideas for places to visit on a return trip. As much as I enjoy visiting the great landmarks, the unplanned stops are as important a part of my travels as the well-known destinations.

CHAPTER 6

Rain, Rain, Go Away

Rain has been an all-too-common part of my baseball games and my travels. In Chapter 11, I will share how a four-hour rain delay kept me as Busch Stadium past 3 am. Years earlier I regretted attending a doubleheader loss at Kauffman Stadium in which the Royals lost two games following a two-hour delay. When driving hundreds of miles in a single day or attending an outdoor event, few things are more frustrating than encountering heavy rain.

My family's first trip outside of visits to grandparents was in 1984, the summer before my sixth-grade year. We spent three nights in Nashville, then drove to New Orleans for the World's Fair. Dad attended college at Loyola University in New Orleans, so he was familiar with the city. Before we arrived at the fair, he mentioned that each afternoon the city predictably received a rainstorm. We were in an outdoor line to enter the Canadian Pavilion and even he was not prepared for that storm. Not only did we receive a torrential downpour heavier than he ever recalled in the city, but the thunder was deafening. In my fear, I nervously asked, "Are we in a hurricane?" The storm passed quickly, although not fast enough for our comfort, and we enjoyed the rest of the fair. The other vivid memory of the day was the irony of the Australian Pavilion set-up—requiring visitors to ride an up escalator to visit the Land Down Under.

Florida is nicknamed the Sunshine State, but my trips have been marked by heavy rain. In the summer of 1990, my family took a trip to Walt Disney World. One of our most vivid memories of Orlando was sitting in the Pizza Hut on International Drive as the water flowed down the atrium window. Later in the trip Disney World had to close the monorail due to thunderstorms. My Florida rain experience is not limited to Orlando. Twenty years later I was planning to attend a baseball game in Clearwater, but scrubbed those plans as my trip down US Highway 19 was marred by ongoing heavy rain. The evening turned out all right as the rain eventually subsided and I watched the sun set over the Gulf of Mexico following dinner at Frenchy's in Clearwater Beach.

Several of my first impressions of states have been marred by rain. My first new state as a solo traveler was West Virginia in the summer of 2006. Coming in on Interstate 64 from Kentucky, I stopped at the West Virginia Welcome Center and was soaked by the time I returned to the car. After stopping at the state capitol, I found myself in heavy rain for much of the drive between Charleston and Morgantown. Two years later I returned to the same welcome center and had another soaking experience. I joked that the state should be renamed Wet Virginia!

Receiving a soggy initial welcome to West Virginia

The day after my West Virginia welcome, wet weather repeated itself in Pennsylvania, which was especially scary as I rounded the sharp curve to remain on Interstate 79 near Washington. Luckily the rain moved out of the area that afternoon and I was able to attend the Pittsburgh Pirates game that evening.

The worst weather I ever encountered in a new state came the following year when I was heading to Michigan for the first time. I had attended the Cubs game at Wrigley Field that afternoon and had already endured Chicago rush hour. The drive through northwest Indiana was especially terrifying. Despite the weather, many vehicles, including large trucks, felt driving at 70 mph was still safe. My car was constantly splashed. Time grew later, and entering Michigan, I lost an hour when I entered the Eastern Time Zone. I stopped at the Michigan Welcome Center on Interstate 94 and learned the area was under a severe thunderstorm warning. Even though the time change put me past 10 pm, I waited a half-hour at the welcome center for the storm to subside before driving the final few miles to Benton Harbor.

One evening a severe weather report shook me up even though I was nowhere near the storms. Knowing that I had a late evening while driving from Cody to Laramie in the summer of 2015, I found the radio to be welcome company. The Wyoming evening seemed pleasant, so when the emergency broadcast signal interrupted programming, I assumed the signal was only a test. However, the National Weather Service had issued a severe thunderstorm warning and I panicked briefly as I could not remember the name of the current county. Just as I was ready to pull to the shoulder and check the atlas, I fortunately passed a county road junction. The blue pentagon road marker showed a different county and I continued to Laramie without weather issues.

One rain encounter cost me an unplanned hotel night. On the last day of my 2008 trip to Baltimore and Philadelphia, I had planned a rare six-state day at the end as I was coming from Pittsburgh. Naturally, at that point I was eager to return home, so I was not thrilled to first see rain on Interstate 70 in western Ohio. An accident at the

Ohio/Indiana border slowed traffic, but allowed me to take a photo of the blue arch over the interstate just inside Ohio. The green signs in Indianapolis announcing Interstate 70 destined toward St. Louis were a welcome sight and I knew I was only four hours from home. Better yet, once I entered Illinois I would gain an hour from the time zone change.

Just west of Indianapolis, I stopped at a Quizno's in Plainfield for a quick dinner. I called my parents to let them know I was in Indiana. Mom told me that due to weather, I should find a hotel and not even try to come home that evening. At that point I just wanted to come home and figured that the time change would offset being slowed by rain. I was wrong as I found out within minutes of re-entering Interstate 70. The rain fell so hard that I pulled to the shoulder for a few minutes as I did not feel I could drive safely under the conditions. Once the rain briefly subsided, before another heavy downpour, I saw a billboard for a Holiday Inn Express at Cloverdale, Indiana, and I counted down the miles to Exit 41. I have seldom been as happy to find a hotel as I was on that soggy night. The next morning I took advantage of the extra day on the road to visit Cataract Falls in Indiana and a former Illinois capitol building in Vandalia.

Rain experiences were not limited to the United States. I had hoped to visit some of the small towns of Québec when driving between Québec and Montreal, but with the rain falling hard, I decided to take the faster Autoroute option.

Severe thunderstorms and rain were not the only unfortunate welcomes to new states. My parents, sister, and I drove to Texas in 2001. As we were leaving the Texas Welcome Center, I was promptly stung by a hornet. Luckily my sister was driving, but I learned not to mess with Texas. On the second day of my first visit to Idaho, my windshield was cracked as I was leaving Idaho Falls. The crack spread during a fast-food lunch in Blackfoot and I worried that the car would not be drivable. Although no glass shop in Blackfoot or Pocatello could replace my windshield that afternoon, one helpful person set me up the next day with an appointment in Boise.

While rain, thunderstorms, a hornet, and a cracked windshield are not my favorite travel memories, these experiences provide a thread of stories that I will remember for years.

CHAPTER 7

Patriotic America

‖‖

Traveling to different cities to watch the Kansas City Royals has allowed me to see many of the great landmarks of the United States. With my traveling time narrowed to the summer months, I am often on vacation on or close to Independence Day. I enjoy visiting the great patriotic landmarks of the United States and in some cases, I have been able to visit these sites on July 4.

In 2008 I attended three Royals games in Baltimore, the dates falling on July 1, 2, and 3. When planning the trip, I noticed that Philadelphia was a short drive from Baltimore and drove to the City of Brotherly Love the morning of Independence Day. It did not hurt that the Phillies were at home that evening, hosting the New York Mets (see Chapter 11).

Just like my first venture into Pennsylvania two years before, I encountered some rain at the welcome center, but the skies cleared enough to enjoy the historic district. My first stop was at the Liberty Bell. No matter how much I heard people talk about the Liberty Bell and no matter how many pictures I had seen, standing next to the famous bell was a special moment, made better because it was the 232nd anniversary of the Declaration of Independence.

After lunch I walked to Independence Hall. Standing in the room where the Declaration of Independence and U. S. Constitution were adopted centuries earlier, I envisioned the debates that took place. I developed new appreciation for the men who developed the early documents of the founding of the United States. Moreover, I became intentional about referring to the anniversary of the Declaration as "Independence Day", instead of casually saying "the fourth of July".

Independence Hall greets a multitude of visitors
on Independence Day 2008.

The 2011 Royals series in Denver also fell on July 1, 2, and 3. Following the last game of the series, I drove to Colorado Springs. The next morning, Independence Day, I rode the cog railway to the top of Pikes Peak. Pikes Peak was the inspiration for Katharine Lee Bates to write the great patriotic hymn *America the Beautiful*. Spending the morning at Pikes Peak, it was easy to see how Bates was moved. The words to *America the Beautiful* floated through my mind that day as the nation celebrated Independence Day. That night I attended the Colorado Springs Sky Sox game and patriotic events from the singing of *The Star-Spangled Banner* to the postgame fireworks were more special after another reminder of the splendor of the United States.

When planning my first visit to New York City in 2013, I had originally hoped to visit the Statue of Liberty on Independence Day. However, the statue was reopening that day after having been closed following Hurricane Sandy and I decided to wait until July 10. The delay did not cost me a sense of wonder. Walking from the subway toward the cruise, I developed goose bumps when the statue first came into view. The Statue of Liberty is even more magnificent up close as I thought about how many people the statue has welcomed to America through the years. Unfortunately, Ellis Island was still closed from hurricane damage, but I would like to visit on a future trip.

Another symbol of the United States—the Statue of Liberty.

The next summer I attended the Royals series in Boston—a city with numerous patriotic sites. I walked the Freedom Trail and attended a presentation in the meeting room of Faneuil Hall. One of my pregame meals was at Quincy Market, located near Faneuil Hall. The Old State House is now home to a Boston history museum. The Minute Man National Historical Park allowed me to walk the battle-fields of Lexington and Concord. Plymouth Rock is located about 40 miles southeast of Boston. The Pilgrim Story in Plymouth, the nation's oldest museum, contains a large collection of 17th century artifacts. After touring the *Mayflower II*, a replica of the original pilgrim ship that sits on the harbor, I was amazed that any colonists survived the voyage from Europe.

On my way home from Boston, I spent two nights in New York. I did not have much sightseeing time as I had acquired a standby ticket for *Late Night with Seth Meyers* and spent much of the day obsessively watching the clock, trying to avoid sweating too much before a possible appearance on national TV. I did have enough time to visit the National September 11 Memorial on the site of the former World Trade Center towers. Occupying the footprint where the two skyscrapers once stood, the two pools with the names of the victims inscribed provided a pow-erful memorial. Meanwhile, the new World Trade Center, then under construction, rose overhead. On my next visit to New York, I would like to visit the museum that opened in 2014.

When I planned my 2008 trip to the eastern seaboard, Fort McHenry was the first attraction I planned for Baltimore. As a student in junior-high choir in the 1980s, I recall memorizing not just the first verse of *The Star-Spangled Banner*, but also the fourth. Visitors to Fort McHenry can obtain copies of all four stanzas. Walking around the fort enabled me to envision what Francis Scott Key encountered in the War of 1812, inspiring him to write the anthem. The video in the visitors center powerfully ended with a rendition of the national anthem while a curtain in the auditorium opened to reveal the flag flying over the fort. Located several miles from Fort McHenry, the Star-Spangled Banner Flag House and Museum is where the flag that inspired Key was sewn.

Rounding a curve on a South Dakota state highway, Mount Rushmore comes into view. No matter how many pictures I had seen of the iconic mountain, there was no substitution for actually visiting Mount Rushmore. Walking paths allow tourists to view the mountain from many angles. The park includes a museum with a display on each U. S. president, not just the four depicted on the mountain, and the Sculptor's Studio was where Gutzon Borglum spent time working on his model. The Evening Lighting Ceremony during the summer months celebrates the four presidents and honors veterans. While visiting Mt. Rushmore, I allowed time to tour the Rushmore Borglum Story in Keystone and saw more of the artist's works. My day in the Black Hills also included a visit to the Crazy Horse Memorial, under construction since 1948.

My visits to Independence Hall, the Liberty Bell, and Pikes Peak were extra special because they fell on Independence Day. Whether Independence Day or any other time of year, these landmarks never fail to stir my patriotism.

CHAPTER 8

Traveling through Time

In the previous chapter, I shared some of the landmarks that stir feelings of patriotism. I still have yet to visit Washington, DC, so I need to tour the U. S. Capitol, the White House, and the National Mall on a future trip. Many landmarks share a slice of American history and provide the opportunity to learn about a historical event in depth.

Valley Forge National Historical Park outside Philadelphia in 2008 was the site of one of my biggest travel mistakes. I had spent much of the day in the central historic district and decided to skip the guided tour, opting for a self-guided driving tour. I have regretted that decision ever since and hope to return for a formal tour. Valley Forge was where General George Washington and the Continental Army camped during the first half of 1778.

My 2009 trip included the major cities of eastern Texas, so I remembered the Alamo in my travel plans. The compound was much smaller than I expected. Although the Mexican troops routed the Texans at the 1836 battle, the Alamo became a rally cry for Texas independence. Less than two months after their defeat at the Alamo, the Texans won a battle near Houston and independence from Mexico was secured.

Although located in present-day West Virginia, Harpers Ferry's claim to fame occurred when the state was still part of Virginia. Less than two years before the Civil War, John Brown led an uprising against slavery and at the time of his hanging, Brown predicted that war was near. The firehouse where Brown resisted the Marines remains and is now called John Brown's Fort. Many other buildings in the historic park depict life in 1859 Harpers Ferry.

The Pony Express delivered mail for less than two years, but its legacy continues at the Pony Express National Museum in St. Joseph, Missouri. Housed in a former stable, exhibits include a blacksmith shop and harness shop. The founders of the short-lived mail route are spotlighted and a map traces the routes west.

When the Royals played a rare series in Atlanta in 2010, I planned my first drive through the Carolinas, with my first South Carolina stop at Fort Sumter. The first shots of the Civil War were fired at the Charleston fort. Visitors arrive at the fort via tour boat, with breathtaking views of the Cooper River and Atlantic Ocean along the way.

The day after my abbreviated trek through Valley Forge, I wisely purchased the bus tour at the Gettysburg National Military Park. Of course, I had studied the Civil War several times in school, but hearing the vivid details of the battle and the events leading to it gave me new appreciation of how many close calls the United States has had in its history. At the time of my visit the Cyclorama was closed while the new museum and visitors center were under construction. The museum was open and displayed thousands of artifacts from the battle. I left the museum thankful for the advances in medicine, surgery, and sanitation that have taken place since 1863. On a future trip through Pennsylvania, I would like to see the Cyclorama.

Normally the first place I set foot on the soil of a new state is a welcome center just inside the state line. Montana was a notable exception when my first stop was at the Little Bighorn National Monument. The visitors center museum tells the story of the 1876 Battle of the Little Bighorn. Narrated by a Native American tour guide, Apsaalooke Tours takes visitors by bus across the battlefield with a thorough description of the events leading up to what is now known as Custer's Last Stand. The site includes both a U. S. Army Memorial and Indian Memorial and individual markers indicate where each person lost his life.

When I was heading home from Denver in 2011, I visited friends who lived in Syracuse, Kansas, providing a perfect opportunity to detour from Interstate 70. The historic town of Dodge City lies just over 100 miles east via US Highway 50. Knowing that I would be sitting in the car for most of the rest of the day, I opted for the Dodge City Trail of Fame walking tour. The businesses feature 1880s western themes and the statue of Wyatt Earp is hard to miss. Dodge City later was the setting for the television western *Gunsmoke*.

Kearney, Nebraska is home to the Great Platte River Road Archway Monument, a museum built above Interstate 80 and one of my favorite stops on my 2015 trip to the Pacific Northwest. Visitors ride an escalator into the bridge and take an audio tour through Nebraska travel history, beginning with the Mormon, Oregon, and California Trails. Subsequent stops include a buffalo stampede, the Transcontinental Railroad, and the Pony Express. The museum continues into 20th century automobile travel, showcasing a Model T car and the Lincoln Highway which crossed Nebraska. A drive-in movie brings visitors into the 1950s. The exhibits conclude with large windows overlooking Interstate 80 underneath representing today's cross-country travel.

Interstate 80 passes underneath the Archway Museum
in Kearney, Nebraska.

One of the most powerful museums I have visited was the National Civil Rights Museum in Memphis. The museum is housed at the Lorraine Motel, where Dr. Martin Luther King was assassinated in 1968. Since I grew up in an integrated community, the burned-out bus and video footage of the fire hoses turned on civil rights marchers were a sobering reminder of the hardships people endured while striving for equality. Quotes from the pro-segregation Southern governors of the era contrast with the election of President Barack Obama a half-century later. A wreath marks the balcony spot where Dr. King was shot. Since I visited in 2012, the museum was remodeled to include more interactive exhibits.

Each state has a history whether focused on the Civil War, the West, colonial history, transportation, industry, or exploration. In Chapter 3, I said that state capitol buildings and presidential libraries are other sources for historical travelers. I always look for opportunities to study history while on the road.

CHAPTER 9

The Great Landmarks

In the previous two chapters I shared my experiences visiting the sites that stir feelings of patriotism and/or tell the story of U. S. history. As I have traveled throughout two countries, I have encountered some of the most recognizable landmarks. These are places that have become iconic within their city or state.

The Gateway Arch in St. Louis is one of the most distinct landmarks in the United States.

I begin with a confession. Even though I have always lived within a 25-mile radius of downtown St. Louis, I have never ridden to the top of the Gateway Arch. The Gateway Arch, of course, is synonymous with St. Louis, incorporated into the logo of numerous media outlets, sports teams, and businesses. As of late 2015, the museum underneath the Arch was closed for an extensive remodeling and expansion, and the park grounds are being extended across a new "lid" over Interstate 44. Once the museum opens, I do plan to visit, and yes, I will finally ride the tram to the observation deck of the 630-foot monument.

There are many places around the St. Louis area from which to photograph the Gateway Arch. I have found that many of the best views of the skyline can be found from the Illinois side. Places to view the Arch and skyline include the parking lot of the Cracker Barrel in Caseyville, the top of Monks Mound at the Cahokia Mounds UNESCO World Heritage Site near Collinsville, and from the parking lot of GCS Ballpark in Sauget. From the Missouri side, Arch views include Missouri Highway 367 from Interstate 270 in North St. Louis County and looking north from Lemay Ferry Road near the South County Center mall. When the St. Louis Cardinals opened their new ballpark in 2006, one of the selling points was that most seats provide views of the Arch.

The Royals series in Toronto in the summer of 2012 provided the opportunity for me to overcome my fear of heights that has kept me from the top of the Gateway Arch. Toronto's CN Tower for decades held the distinction as the world's tallest tower and still remains the highest in North America. I opted for the lower of the two observation decks, which still included riding an elevator 1122 feet. The deck provided outstanding views of Toronto and Lake Ontario. More adventurous visitors may choose the SkyPod at 1465 feet. The bravest guests may choose the EdgeWalk, a tethered outdoor walk 1168 feet above ground. I must admit that watching EdgeWalk commercials during the Blue Jays games left me nervous, so I will definitely pass on that experience.

Having conquered my fear of heights at the CN Tower, I had no qualms visiting the Space Needle in Seattle three years later. Like the Gateway Arch in St. Louis, the Space Needle is symbolic of Seattle. Its circular observation deck is 520 feet high and offers spectacular views of Seattle, Mount Rainier, and Puget Sound. One surprise on the observation deck was a free photograph that could be immediately shared on Facebook; by the time I returned to my hotel room, dozens of people had already "liked" the photo. A concession stand is available on the observation deck; the Space Needle also offers an elegant restaurant. I was there in mid-morning and snacked on a bag of the local Tim's Potato Chips.

Most of my major trip routes form sweeping loops so I can see more places. For instance, my 2011 trip to Denver included a route across western South Dakota and down the eastern side of Wyoming. With my enthusiasm for visiting Mount Rushmore, Crazy Horse, and Wall Drug, I nearly overlooked Devils Tower. I would have regretted that oversight, given that the first U. S. national monument is located minutes off Interstate 90 in northeast Wyoming. A visitor center offers exhibits describing the history of the area and its importance to Native Americans.

Yellowstone National Park sits on the opposite side of Wyoming. On my way home from Seattle in 2015, I knew I wanted to see Old Faithful erupt. However, Yellowstone consists of much more than just geysers. Several weeks before my trip I learned about the Grand Prismatic Spring as the second place to visit within the park. However, once I entered Yellowstone, I discovered the park had many more wondrous attractions. I attempted a selfie at the 45th parallel marker, just north of the Montana/Wyoming border. As I drove through the park I added stops at a visitor center, several waterfalls, and other geysers and scenic overlooks. After driving around desperately trying to find a parking space at Old Faithful, I arrived at the famed geyser only ten minutes before its expected eruption. The eruption was magnificent, a sight to behold. Even though I spent more time searching for a parking space than the eruption actually lasted, the beauty of Old

Faithful overrides parking-lot frustrations. My Yellowstone day turned into a lengthy adventure as I will share in Chapter 22.

As its name implied, Old Faithful erupted right on schedule. That was the last time the drive from Bozeman to Laramie remained on schedule.

Vancouver became the first and so far, only Winter Olympics host city I have visited. The Olympic Cauldron on Vancouver Harbour stands as a reminder of the 2010 games and is periodically lit for special events. The torch is located behind the Vancouver Convention Centre and was an easy walk from the Waterfront Station. While strolling through downtown Vancouver, I enjoyed dinner at the Steamworks Brewing Company adjacent to the light-rail station.

When I was talking with local fans at Safeco Field, I joked that I was the "stereotypical Seattle tourist", having visited the Pike Place Market and Space Needle within 24 hours of arriving in the city. However, any first-time visit to Seattle must include both attractions. Wyoming advertises Devils Tower and Old Faithful on billboards in a number of states, including Missouri. The Gateway Arch and CN Tower define the skylines of their respective cities. The Vancouver Olympic Cauldron stands as a reminder of a successful sporting event that brought international attention to the western Canadian city. Even though these are not unique travel experiences, I am glad to have visited each landmark.

CHAPTER 10

Let the Water Fall

||||||||||||||||||||||||||||||||||||||||||||||||||||||||||||||||||||||||||||||||||||||||||||||||||||||||||||||||||||||||||||||||||||||||||||||||||||||||||

Waterfalls are among nature's most majestic landmarks. The sheer volume of water rushing over the ledge is breathtaking. Niagara Falls is an internationally known waterfall, but I have found other great waterfalls, two of which were stops not on my original itinerary.

My 2008 trip home from the eastern seaboard was marred by a rainstorm on what was supposed to be the final day (see Chapter 6). The positive aspect to spending the unplanned night in Cloverdale, Indiana was the opportunity the next day to visit two additional attractions. I intended to visit the former Illinois capitol building in Vandalia, but as so often happens when I travel, another stop crept into the day's plans.

Signs near my Cloverdale hotel promoted the nearby Cataract Falls, located in the Lieber State Recreation Area. The area around the waterfall included Owen County's only surviving covered bridge. Cataract Falls at 45 feet is shorter than most waterfalls, but their beauty led me to discover other waterfalls on later trips. The "bonus" stops that day cancelled my irritation over delaying my return home.

Dad and I drove through the Upper Midwest and eastern Plains in 2009, with one of the items on our mutual bucket list the Corn Palace in Mitchell, South Dakota. We spent the previous evening in Sioux Falls and naturally wanted to see the city's namesake. When we were there, the park hosted a laser light show featuring the region's history, but unfortunately, the program has since been discontinued. The park includes a 50-foot observation tower with views of the city and falls.

In 2010 I was in Minneapolis to attend my first baseball game at Target Field. I was starting to feel old as I had remembered riding the bus past the construction site of the Twins previous stadium, the Hubert H. Humphrey Metrodome, when I was a young boy. During my grandparents' lifetimes, we had so much fun dining, shopping, and playing together, that I had not seen many of the Twin Cities better-known tourist attractions. One such place was Minnehaha Falls, a name that stood out in my family as my grandparents lived for decades on Minnehaha Avenue in St. Paul. At 53 feet, Minnehaha Falls is slightly taller than Cataract Falls. The falls achieved fame when Henry Wadsworth Longfellow wrote his famous poem *The Song of Hiawatha*.

The most notable falls, of course, are Niagara Falls. When MLB released its 2012 schedule and I decided to attend the Royals series in Toronto, I knew that Niagara Falls would be a must-visit for two reasons. First, I had heard from many people that the best views of the falls were from the Canadian side. (I did not enter New York on that trip.) Second, I knew people who had gone to Toronto and regretted not knowing they were close to Niagara Falls and I would not repeat their mistake.

The weather looked ominous, so instead of the Maid of the Mist cruise, I opted to walk through the Journey Behind the Falls. Visitors wear disposable raincoats and walk through passageways, enabling them to stand behind the falling water of Horseshoe Falls. Long sidewalks offer numerous angles for photographing the falls. I attended a film at the IMAX Theatre that shared the history of people who attempted to roll over the falls in a barrel. On the walk back to my car, rain poured so hard that I wished I still had my raincoat from Journey Behind the Falls. The rain soaked me much more than my journey close to the actual falls and I drove back to Toronto grateful that the Blue Jays played in a stadium with a retractable roof.

Horseshoe Falls of Niagara Falls, taken from the Ontario side.
Notice the rain clouds moving into the area.

Montmorency Falls, located just outside Quebec City, are actually taller than Niagara Falls. Water flows into the St. Lawrence River. After spending a day exploring the historic district of Quebec and touring the province's parliament building, I drove to the falls. Like with Niagara Falls, Montmorency offers many different locations to view the falls. I surprised myself by riding a cable-suspended car, but was rewarded at the top with spectacular views of the falls. A pedestrian bridge allows visitors to stand over the falls.

As I mentioned earlier, when attending the Idaho Falls Chukars baseball game, I admitted to other fans that it was my first visit to Idaho. I even confessed that I had to learn what a chukar was—and even the correct pronunciation of "chukar". When hearing that I was driving to Boise the next day, one fan told me to be sure to stop at Shoshone Falls, located near Twin Falls. Nicknamed the "Niagara of the West", Shoshone Falls is also taller than Niagara, with water flowing into the Snake River. Admission to the park was a bargain at $3 per car, and admiring the beauty of the area distracted me from the day's broken windshield incident on Interstate 15. I am grateful to the Chukars fan for his advice, otherwise I probably would have missed one of the West's great natural wonders.

When I vacationed in Boston in the summer of 2014, I attended church at Aldersgate United Methodist Church in nearby Worcester, Massachusetts. The opening hymn that Sunday was *For the Beauty of the Earth* and if memory serves me correctly, we sang each of the six verses with a different organ setting. Visiting the different waterfalls of the U. S. and Canada, along with viewing other natural attractions like mountains, oceans, geysers, and rolling hills, remind me that North America is filled with beauty.

CHAPTER 11

Making Major-League Memories

Baseball lends itself to storytelling. I have attended professional baseball games at over 35 major- and minor-league stadiums, some of which have fallen to the wrecking ball. Stadiums are a good way to meet local people and learn about their cities.

I enjoy discovering what makes each ballpark unique. When I saw the Royals face Felix Hernandez at Safeco Field, a section called King Felix's Court chanted, "K, K, K, K, K, K..." each time he reached two strikes on a batter. Singing *Take Me Out to the Ballgame* at Wrigley Field is an emotional experience. Fans at the ballparks in Houston and Arlington sing *Deep in the Heart of Texas* and Frank Sinatra's *New York, New York* follows each game at Yankee Stadium. Great American Ball Park honors its location on the Ohio River with a steamboat motif.

Despite their reputation for arrogance, I found the fans at Yankee Stadium to be down-to-earth. Some even laugh about the stereotype while proving that it is not true. One fan quizzed me on who gave up Chris Chambliss's walkoff home run against the Royals in the 1976 playoffs. I had to think for a minute as I was still in preschool before answering with Mark Littell. My correct answer earned the fan's respect and we had good conversation throughout the game.

When possible, I try to schedule games in which I have no vested interest. Those games are enjoyable because five minutes after the last out, the final score will not have mattered to me. I am probably one of the few Midwesterners who has seen the San Diego Padres play interleague games against both the Texas Rangers and Tampa Bay Rays.

Telling all my baseball stories would require a set of volumes, but I have a few favorites.

Seitzer's perfect day
Royals Stadium—August 2, 1987

Dad and I took our first father-son trip to Kansas City in the summer of 1987. With temperatures rising over 100 degrees, fans baked in the stands, but the players were even hotter playing on the Astroturf that was common in 1980s stadiums. Royals third baseman Kevin Seitzer, a candidate for Rookie of the Year in any year other than when Mark McGwire was smashing records, came up to bat in the bottom of the eighth inning with runners on second and third and the Royals leading the Red Sox 7-3. Seitzer had already collected five hits in the game and Dad asked me if Boston would intentionally walk the hot hitter. I reminded him that with future Hall of Famer George Brett on deck, the Red Sox would likely pitch to Seitzer. Indeed they did, and he responded by sending a pitch over right fielder Mike Greenwell's head that bounced into the stands for a ground-rule double and his sixth hit. An intentional walk would not have worked better for the Red Sox as George Brett followed with a home run. Seitzer's 6-for-6 game is still the rarest feat I have seen in a major-league game and cemented my loyalty to the Royals.

Schmidt happens
Busch Stadium—October 10, 2002

While not a road trip for me, this was my first National League Championship Series game. I attended with my friend Justin who transplanted from Pittsburgh and was a long-time fan of Barry Bonds. He had been encouraging me to treat myself to a playoff game and we selected Game 2. The game was most memorable for the dominance of San Francisco Giants pitcher Jason Schmidt in their 4-1 win, which led me to deliver the quip, "Schmidt happens". My friend has reminded me of that phrase many times since. The Giants later advanced to their first World Series since 1989.

500 home runs for Griffey
Busch Stadium—June 20, 2004

Another memorable game that did not require much time on the road came in the 2004 season. Two friends and I wanted to celebrate a graduation at the ballpark and one observed that the Reds would be coming into town in mid-June with Ken Griffey, Jr. closing in on 500 career home runs. We decided to attend the Father's Day afternoon game and sure enough, Griffey entered with 499 blasts. The game was largely uneventful until Griffey led off the top of the sixth with his milestone shot. At the time, we did not realize that Griffey's dad was at the game for his special moment. Even though the home team lost, fans left with a moment they will remember for a lifetime. Several weeks later I traveled to Cincinnati for the first time and bought a T-shirt commemorating Griffey's day in history.

Independence Day walkoff
Citizens Bank Park—July 4, 2008

Following a Royals series in Baltimore in which Alex Gordon homered onto Eutaw Street, I arrived in Philadelphia the morning of Independence Day. That evening the Phillies hosted the New York Mets. I was surprised by the number of Mets fans, not realizing the two cities were only 100 miles apart. Soon I learned just how bitter the rivalry was when my section cheered loudly as an intoxicated Mets fan was removed from the seating area. The night's pitching matchup appeared to heavily favor the Mets. Former Cy Young Award winner Johan Santana opposed JA Happ, who has had a respectable major-league career, but had just been recalled from the minor leagues. However, the game entered the bottom of the ninth inning tied 2-2.

Phillies sluggers Ryan Howard and Pat Burrell struck out, giving the Phillies two out and nobody on base, just as a few drops of rain began to fall. Extra innings and possibly a rain delay appeared inevitable.

Pedro Feliz delivered a two-out double and Shane Victorino followed with an RBI single for the Phillies win. The Phillies fans boisterously celebrated as the stadium's replica Liberty Bell clanged. Several months later the Phillies completed an improbable run to the championship and having experienced their sports passion, I envisioned what the euphoria must have been when the Phillies fielded the final out of the World Series.

Moose grand in Canada
Rogers Centre—July 2, 2012

When driving in the northern states and Canada, each time I see a "Moose Crossing" sign, I always say "MOOOOOOOOOOSE". Beginning with his first Triple-A home run in a 2010 game at Memphis, Royals third baseman Mike Moustakas has been a dependable performer in games I attend. Although the Rogers Centre was mostly empty, my section was spirited, as the usher led the Toronto fans in chants like "Colby [Rasmus], HIT, HIT, HIT" when the Blue Jays batted. The Royals held a 7-3 lead in the top of the seventh when Moustakas belted his first career grand slam and Kansas City finished with an 11-3 win.

This story has two follow-ups. A year later I was walking around downtown Cooperstown near the Baseball Hall of Fame and encountered people wearing Royals jerseys. We began discussing games and I remarked that I would be at the Royals series at Yankee Stadium the following week. One person then asked if I had been at the series in Toronto the previous year—he had actually remembered me from Canada! In September 2014 I met Moustakas at a Kansas City area sports store and had the chance to tell him that I had seen what was then his lone career slam in person (his second slam came in September 2015).

Working around the clock
Busch Stadium—May 30, 2013

Although a local game for me, arriving home after 4 am the next morning felt like returning from a long road trip. The hometown crowd eagerly anticipated the game as the highly-touted pitcher Michael

Wacha was making his major-league debut for St. Louis. After a one-hour rain delay, the game started and Wacha pitched superbly, with the Cardinals leading 2-1 after eight innings. As the game entered the ninth inning, rain began falling and I heard a frustrated St. Louis fan exclaim, "That is God saying he does not want [reliever] Mitchell Boggs in this game!" Sure enough, Royals outfielder Jeff Francouer promptly tied the game with a leadoff home run. Eric Hosmer later delivered a two-run single to give the Royals a 4-2 lead.

After an intentional walk, the rain fell even harder and the grounds crew quickly brought out the tarp again. Meanwhile, the night grew later and later, but I could not pass up the opportunity to see the end of a Royals win. I received a text from a friend in Kansas City at 1:30 am, saying he had just seen me on TV. Finally, the rain stopped shortly after 2 am. While the grounds crew readied the field, the Royals players were having fun, signing autographs and tossing bags of peanuts to their fans. Since the crowd of nearly 44,000 had dwindled to nearly 100 or so fans, each team's faithful stood behind their respective dugouts. The game resumed at 3:02 am and the stadium was so empty that we could hear every word broadcast by longtime Cardinal announcer Mike Shannon. The Royals had been struggling the past few days and I had visions of the Cardinals tying the game and forcing extra innings. Greg Holland finally recorded the last out at 3:14 am, sending the tired fans home.

Two years later I attended a game in Kansas City that began with an unexpected rain delay. To pass time while waiting out the weather, I bought a copy of Royals General Manager Dayton Moore's book *More Than a Season*. Toward the end of the book (p. 165-166), Moore wrote that he believed the come-from-behind win started the Royals on their improved play that ultimately led to the 2014 American League championship.

Overtime work on the holiday
Citi Field—July 4, 2013

The Mets hosted the Arizona Diamondbacks in their final home game before a long road trip while Citi Field was readied for the

2013 All-Star Game. Having just arrived in New York the night before, I was hoping that after the game I would have time to shop the legendary Macy's at Herald Square and dine at Katz's Deli. Inside Citi Field I picked up lunch at Shake Shack before watching a game that was most memorable for its length. The Mets and Diamondbacks remained tied 2-2 until Arizona scored on a bases-loaded walk in the top of the 13th inning. I was about ready to head for the subway when Mets catcher Anthony Recker homered to tie the game with two out. Arizona jumped back ahead in the 14th for a 4-3 lead. Before the Mets came up to bat in the bottom of the 14th, fans sang *Take Me Out to the Ballgame* for the Fourteenth Inning Stretch. With one out, Kirk Nieuwenheis homered to tie the game again. Arizona shortstop Cliff Pennington delivered an RBI single for a 5-4 Diamondback lead in the 15th inning. The Mets put the tying run on third and winning run on second in the bottom of the inning and I was sure we were headed to yet another extra inning. The Diamondbacks escaped the jam to end a game that lasted nearly six hours.

Although Macy's had to wait until the following week, the long game gave me the chance to appreciate how New York is truly The City That Never Sleeps. Despite the late evening on Independence Day, I was still able to enjoy my Katz's Deli sandwich that evening.

Opening Day as the American League champs
Kauffman Stadium—April 6, 2015

As a Royals fan living in eastern Missouri, I was constantly reminded of the team's lengthy stretch of futility that was finally snapped with a trip to 2014 World Series. Opening Day 2015 fell on Easter Monday, a school holiday, and I decided this might be a once-in-a-lifetime opportunity to see a pennant raised in Kansas City. Before the game, the players received their World Series rings as the team raised the 2014 American League championship banner for the first time. The celebration continued as the Kansas City Symphony performed *The Star-Spangled Banner*. Not content to rest on their laurels, the Royals opened the season by defeating the Chicago White Sox 10-1 as Mike Moustakas and Alex Rios homered. I did not know this at the time, but I would later see the American League championship banner raised in another stadium two months later.

Not every baseball story is memorable for a good reason. I was at a sparsely-attended 2004 doubleheader in which the Royals were swept by the Montreal Expos following a lengthy rain delay. I have sat in the stands through blowouts and games in which neither team was throwing strikes. Walkoff home runs are fun when you are cheering for the home team and torture when rooting for the visitors. Every time I attend a ballgame I wonder if I will see history made.

The beginning of exploring unfamiliar cities as a solo traveler began with a 2005 win in Cleveland. At the time, the Indians stadium was called Jacobs Field.

Two years after I saw Ken Griffey Jr's 500th career home run, the Royals were victimized by his 552nd. The steamboat motif and location on the Ohio River make Great American Ball Park one of the best 21st century stadiums.

Tigers outfielder Curtis Granderson faced the Royals in a 2007 game at Comerica Park. Granderson hit 3 home runs in the 2015 World Series.

Alex Gordon, a rookie third baseman wearing #7, bats for the Royals in a 2007 game at the Hubert H. Humphrey Metrodome in Minneapolis.

Paul Konerko leads off first base with Luke Hochevar pitching in a June 2008 game at US Cellular Field. Six years later I attended another Royals game in Chicago when the White Sox honored Konerko's career.

The Royals shake hands following a 2008 win at Camden Yards. Earlier in the series Alex Gordon sent a home run to Eutaw Street.

The author meets then-manager Trey Hillman before a 2009 Zack Greinke
start in Houston. Greinke dominated that night in his Cy Young season.
Leaving Houston was remembered for breaking news of a celebrity death.

One of the few times the Royals faced Chipper Jones was in a 2010 game
in Atlanta. Turner Field will be replaced following the 2016 season.

Royals rookie third baseman Mike Moustakas signs autographs
and greets fans before a 2011 game at Coors Field.

The author chats with Royals pitcher Bruce Chen before a 2012 game
on a hot evening in Toronto.

The Royals celebrate their 4-2 win in St. Louis at 3:14 am in 2013.
Dayton Moore cited this game as the beginning of the Royals
return to respectability.

Salvador Perez bats at Yankee Stadium in 2013. Notice the rain clouds
moving in—true to my travel form, we ended up in a delay. The Royals
won that evening and split the four-game series in New York.

Danny Duffy pitches to David Ortiz with the Green Monster looming
in a 2014 game at historic Fenway Park.

Raising the 2014 American League champions banner
on Opening Day 2015 at Kauffman Stadium.

May 29, 2015 marked the Royals first trip to Wrigley Field in nearly 14 years. The wait was worthwhile for Royals fans as the visitors pulled out an 8-4 win.

Notice the large number of Royals fans sitting behind the visiting dugout before a June 2015 game at Safeco Field in Seattle.

An unsuspecting Royal gets an ice-water bath following
an August 2015 win at Kauffman Stadium.

Following the Royals 2010 series in Atlanta, I drove to St. Petersburg and
saw the Rays host the Padres. Wade Davis, who pitched the last inning
of the 2015 World Series, is facing Adrian Gonzalez.

CHAPTER 12

Major Fun in the Minors

|||||||||||||||||||||||||||||||||||||||||||||||||||||||||||||||||||||||||||||||||||||||||||||||||||||||||||||||||||||||||||||||||||||||||||||||||||

Minor-league baseball is an underrated form of entertainment. For a ticket price comparable to a movie, you can often see future major-league stars. I watched All-Star closer Greg Holland pitch in a Class-A game in Wilmington, Delaware in 2008. Two

The minor leagues often have first-rate mascots.
Sox the Fox welcomed the author to Colorado Springs.

years later I saw Mike Moustakas hit his first AAA home run shortly after his promotion to Omaha. Sometimes you catch an established major-leaguer on an injury rehabilitation assignment such as when I watched Shane Victorino, of walkoff fame from my 2008 Philadelphia trip, play in Pawtucket. Most of the minor-league teams have mascots that are more entertaining than their major-league counterparts and in many parks, it is easy to get your picture taken with the mascot. Some of the ballparks even have great food options, with Frontier Field, home of the Rochester Red Wings, especially notable for its specialty macaroni and cheese, among other menu items.

The no-hitter that wasn't
Auto Zone Park—July 18, 2011

Dad has reminded me many times that he has never seen a no-hitter in person, even though he once saw something rarer—an unassisted triple play. We were in Memphis, watching the host Redbirds face the Omaha Storm Chasers in a battle of the Triple-A affiliates of the Missouri teams. Omaha pitcher Luis Mendoza carried a no-hitter into the bottom of the ninth inning. The first Redbird batter, Tyler Greene, led off with a deep fly ball that the left fielder narrowly missed. I quickly wrote 2B on my scorecard as there was little doubt in my mind that the play was a legitimate double. Dad pointed out to me that the scoreboard showed an error and the no-hitter was intact. No subsequent Redbird reached base as the Storm Chasers finished their 4-0 win. Although I had seen high-school pitchers hurl no-hitters, Dad and I drove back from Memphis thinking we had both seen our first professional no-hitter. Not so fast. Two days later the Pacific Coast League awarded Greene the double and Mendoza was denied his no-no. To this day Dad has still never seen a no-hitter in person.

Raising another American League flag
Melaleuca Field—June 18, 2015

The Idaho Falls season opener was one for the Chukars to forget as the home team fell behind 16-2 before scoring eight unanswered runs. As a Royals fan from Missouri, though, the evening had a special moment before the game. Just as I saw the Royals do on their Opening Day in April, the Chukars commemorated their affiliation by raising a 2014 American League pennant. On my way home, I also saw the American League pennant flying over Werner Park in Omaha.

Having entered Idaho for the first time only a few hours earlier, I learned more about the area by chatting with fans. One fan told me to make sure I ate French fries at least once while in Idaho. I admitted that I had thought about potatoes, but was afraid to bring up the subject, lest the natives thought I was stereotyping the state. I was encouraged to visit not only the local falls, but also to stop at Shoshone Falls en route to Boise (see Chapter 10).

A series of coincidences
Memorial Stadium—June 20, 2015

I had scheduled seven baseball games on my trip to the Pacific Northwest—three in Seattle, one in Kansas City, one in Tacoma, one in Idaho Falls, and one in Omaha. After a long Monday through Friday in which I had trekked from St. Louis to Boise, I decided to take advantage of a hotel deal and spend two nights in Boise. After replacing my windshield and visiting the Idaho State Capitol, I had some much-needed Saturday afternoon relaxation time at the hotel. The thought hit me that maybe I should see the Hawks play as long I was in Boise anyway.

Driving to the stadium, I was thinking the Hawks were still a Chicago Cubs affiliate, forgetting that they had switched to the Colorado Rockies for the 2015 season. Three weeks earlier Matt Meier, whose stats I had kept in a men's baseball league a few years prior, was drafted in the 30th round by the Rockies. Meier signed with the Rockies on June 16, the second day of my trip, as I drove from

Sioux City, Iowa to Gillette, Wyoming. I was unaware that the Rockies had assigned him to their Class-A club in Boise. So it was quite the surprise to see Meier's name on the Hawks roster and he was stunned to see a familiar face from Missouri approach the bullpen area prior to the game. Neither of us had ever been to Boise prior to that week so our unplanned reunion was a pleasant surprise.

Neither the author nor Boise Hawks pitcher Matt Meier
expected to see each other that evening.

One last game worth mentioning was a 2009 NCAA Division III college game in Mt. Vernon, Iowa. I had driven to watch a graduate of my district's high school play his Senior Day baseball games for Cornell College. The host Rams trailed Loras College 17-8 entering the bottom of the seventh. Cornell rallied for ten runs in their last at-bat for an improbable 18-17 comeback victory, proving once again that no matter what level of baseball, anything can happen during a trip to the ballpark.

CHAPTER 13

Good Sports

My sports tourism has not been limited to the stadiums and arenas. As I have traveled across the United States and Canada, I have discovered a number of sports museums, some internationally famous and others known only locally. Sports fans will enjoy visiting any of these museums and shrines.

Cooperstown, New York tops many baseball fans' bucket lists for good reason. Fans of all 30 major-league teams will find artifacts of interest at the National Baseball Hall of Fame and Museum. Fortunately, I planned to spend the entire day in Cooperstown, a town located 15 miles off the interstate via a two-lane road. After spending two days in New York City, I was surprised how rural the area around Cooperstown is. As I drove New York Highway 28 toward the town, I smelled manure associated with drives through Midwest farm territory.

Memorabilia spanning the entire history of baseball from the legend of Abner Doubleday to the present-day stars is displayed at the Hall of Fame. I saw the helmet Ken Griffey Jr. wore when he belted his 500th career home run, bringing back memories of the June 2004 afternoon at Busch Stadium. A partial list of artifacts include the baseballs of Hank Aaron's 714th career home run and the record-breaking 756th for Barry Bonds, a pinwheel from the old Comiskey Park scoreboard, a ticket stub from the infamous 1919 World Series, jerseys of nearly every legendary player, midget Eddie Gaedel's ⅛ jersey from a St. Louis Browns stunt, and the ball from the last out of the 2004 World Series when the Boston Red Sox ended their 86-year drought. Each of the 30 teams has a "locker" with jerseys, shoes, gloves, bats, and balls from great moments in their history. Numerous baseball cards are displayed including the expensive T-206 Honus Wagner cigarette card and the 1951 Bowman Mickey Mantle rookie card. The museum ends with the gallery displaying plaques of all the Hall of Famers.

Visitors should allow time to walk around downtown Cooperstown and eat lunch at a local, non-chain restaurant. Many stores are baseball-themed, selling cards, autographs, clothing, and other memorabilia. Parking downtown is limited, but the Cooperstown Trolley operates from three locations with ample parking on the edges of town.

Unlike its baseball counterpart, the Pro Football Hall of Fame is located right off Interstate 77 in Canton, Ohio. Given the recent discussions of the impact of football on the players' long-term health, I was stunned to discover just how primitive the safety gear was for much of the 20th century. Each NFL team has a display covering the great moments of its history and another showcase recounts each Super Bowl. Busts of each member of the Hall of Fame are displayed.

On the outside, the Naismith Memorial Basketball Hall of Fame in Springfield, Massachusetts appears less like a shrine and more like a strip mall. I thought I was at the wrong place since the first thing I noticed was a Subway restaurant. Like the baseball and football museums, the building covers the entire history of basketball from peach baskets to the college game to the NBA and WNBA to international competition. The museum emphasizes interactivity with plenty of opportunities to shoot hoops on the main floor.

Josh Pahigian wrote a 2008 book called *101 Baseball Places to See Before You Strike Out*, a useful guide for baseball tourists. One hundred of the venues were in the United States, the lone exception was the Canadian Baseball Hall of Fame in the charming town of St. Marys, Ontario. The Toronto Blue Jays and gone-but-not-forgotten

Montreal Expos are featured prominently. I had forgotten that a number of superstar players were Canadian, including Hall of Famer Fergie Jenkins and 2006 American League Most Valuable Player Justin Morneau.

Back in the United States, baseball fans can watch bats under construction at the Louisville Slugger Museum & Factory. A wall displays each major-league player who has had his name branded onto a Louisville Slugger bat. Each guest receives a miniature souvenir bat. Visitors may also order personalized bats.

Springfield, Missouri is home to the Missouri Sports Hall of Fame. This museum thoroughly covers the four pro sports teams that call Missouri home, along with the former Kansas City Kings, St. Louis football Cardinals, and St. Louis Rams. As a lifelong Missourian, I recalled many of the players' careers, but had forgotten that many major-league baseball players were natives of the Show-Me State. College and high school sports are also showcased.

Probably the most infamous drain cover in baseball history

An unexpected stop on my 2011 trip to Denver was the National Ballpark Museum, formerly B's Ballpark Museum, about a block from Coors Field. This museum is dedicated to the stadiums themselves and founder Bruce Hellerstein loves to share the stories behind the memorabilia. The museum includes seats from many stadiums of the past, a Yankee Stadium turnstile, the Forbes Field cornerstone, and part of Fenway Park's Green Monster. When I visited the museum, Hellerstein most enjoyed talking about the Yankee Stadium drainage cover where Mickey Mantle tripped and injured his leg during the 1951 World Series.

In October 2015 I fulfilled a dream of finally attending a playoff game at Kauffman Stadium. The extra trip to Kansas City allowed me to finally return to the Negro Leagues Baseball Museum. The museum sits at 18th and Vine, between the stadium and downtown. Founded in part by former Kansas City Monarch Buck O'Neill, the museum intertwines Negro League history with United States civil rights history. James Earl Jones narrates the introductory video. Josh Gibson and Satchel Paige are prominently featured among other Negro League legends. One visitor remarked to me that he was even more impressed with this museum than the Baseball Hall of Fame because the displays tell a story, instead of just displaying artifacts. For the drive home I bought a CD in the gift shop consisting of interviews with O'Neill.

I would like to revisit the Field of Dreams in Dyersville, Iowa, which I last saw in 1994. Many major-league baseball teams now have museums inside their stadiums, most notably Monument Park at Yankee Stadium, and they provide a way to learn about the franchise history or at least walk down Memory Lane.

Since the late 1980s, my favorite athlete outside baseball has been Michael Jordan. Thus I knew that after visiting the capitol in Raleigh in 2010, I would be stopping in Chapel Hill to visit the Carolina Basketball Museum. Jordan is featured prominently, as well as other Tar Heel legends such as James Worthy, Dean Smith, and Missouri native Tyler Hansbrough.

I have been a Kansas City Royals fan for decades, but I enjoy learning about the other teams, as well. On my next trip to Toronto, I would like to visit the Hockey Hall of Fame. As I travel, I meet many other people who share my passion for baseball. Each sport has been shaped by so many people through the years, and each of these sites tells their stories.

CHAPTER 14

Taking a Bite Out of the Big Apple

|||||||||||||||||||||||||||||||||||||||||||||||||||||||||||||||||||||||||||||||||||||||||||||||||||||||||||||||||||||||||||||||||||||||||||||||||||||||||||||||||||

When the 2013 MLB schedule was released the previous September, the Royals summer games included only one ballpark I had not yet visited—Yankee Stadium. Since New York is more than twice as large as any other city in the U. S. or Canada, I must admit I was apprehensive. I convinced myself to take the trip, knowing that any plans to visit all 30 ballparks had to include both Citi Field and Yankee Stadium. Since the Mets were about to embark on a long road trip, I broke my time in New York into two parts so I could visit both stadiums.

I was scheduled to arrive in New York on Wednesday, July 3 with plans to attend that evening's Mets game. My day was to begin at the New Jersey State House, but that morning I discovered that after 8000 photos, my digital camera had worn out. I asked a Trenton police officer if he knew of a nearby Best Buy store; I ended up taking an unexpected detour into Pennsylvania to buy a new camera before returning to tour the capitol. As mentioned earlier, I encountered rain, traffic, and a one-hour wait in line at Carlo's Bake Shop. All day I was asking myself if I was really going to be in New York City later that day. After driving through the Holland Tunnel during rush hour, I was indeed in Manhattan and moments later I crossed the Brooklyn Bridge as I searched for my hotel, located in an industrial area of Brooklyn.

As I drove toward Citi Field, my bearings became completely twisted and I remember making several wrong turns on the area highways and parkways. Worse yet, but not surprising since New York was a new state, rain started falling and traffic was heavy and finally I decided that I could not make it to the stadium in time and I would wait until the next day to see the Mets host the Diamondbacks (see Chapter 11). The lone highlight of the evening was encountering a rainbow on my drive back to the hotel. I was tired, wet, irritated, and thinking that traveling to New York was a mistake.

The next day was spent with a much longer visit to Citi Field than I had planned, followed by a late dinner at Katz's Deli. I began using the subway system, which at first I found confusing. I kept asking people for directions and probably asked every question except, "Can you tell me how to get, how to get to Sesame Street?" I was glad the next day I would be leaving New York City, driving north to visit the Franklin D. Roosevelt Museum, the state capitol, and the Baseball Hall of Fame over the next two days. After my initial experiences, I was dreading returning for the Royals/Yankees series. The one thing I kept reminding myself was that millions of tourists love visiting the Big Apple each year and there were probably good reasons why.

After contrasting the rest of New York State with its largest city, I returned on Sunday, July 7. My hotel in Queens was located within walking distance of the 7 subway line, which I first used to attend the off-Broadway musical *Avenue Q* that evening.

When I reached street level from the subway station, I looked around and noticed buildings such as the World's Largest Applebee's. I thought to myself that this was how I envisioned New York City, then continued to survey my surroundings. I realized I had found Times Square! Having watched Dick Clark and later Ryan Seacrest count down the seconds to the new year many times, I was excited by my discovery. Even though Clark had died the previous year, when I stood in Times Square, I could practically hear him counting down the time. Some of the unusual retailers like the Hershey's Store and M&M Store immediately grabbed my attention.

I knew that to experience New York, I should attend a show and had recently read about *Avenue Q*, performing at New World Stages on West 50th Street. *Avenue Q* was a hilarious musical, definitely NOT family-friendly, that uses *Sesame Street*-style puppets and human characters to address real-world topics such as financial and relationship struggles and finding one's purpose.

The Royals series at Yankee Stadium opened the next evening. However, many New York City attractions are closed on Mondays. About a month earlier, I put the question on my Facebook wall about what I should do, see, or eat in New York. One of the best pieces of advice I received came from one of my former high-school teachers, who suggested taking a Gray Line tour. That seemed easy, now that I knew the way to Times Square.

The Gray Line tour enabled me to see far more of Manhattan than I could have realistically explored on my own. The bus traveled past the United Nations, several luxury hotels, near Wall Street, past Madison Square Garden, through Chinatown, and around the edge of Central Park. As we passed the homes of CBS, ABC, Fox, and HBO I realized just how important a media center New York is. The tour guide included many pop culture references to the local attractions; otherwise, I would have never known to visit Magnolia Bakery. Best yet, I finally understood that with the exceptions of the two ballparks, most of New York's important tourist venues are clustered in Manhattan, not spread over all five boroughs.

While the Royals and Yankees were splitting their four-game series, I came to join the millions of people worldwide who love New York City. I toured the Museum of Modern Art, most notably seeing Andy Warhol's *Campbell's Soup Cans* and Claude Monet's *Water Lilies*. The next day I visited the Statue of Liberty and enjoyed New York-style pizza at Ray's Pizza. One thing I remember about the Gray Line tour guide was him emphatically saying, "Don't come to New York and eat at McDonald's." Ray's Pizza was an enjoyable, less-expensive option with garlic knots a delicious side order.

Andy Warhol could turn ordinary soup cans into a great work of art.

On my last full day in New York, prior to the afternoon baseball game, I made a decision that ended up impacting my next summer's major trip. NBC offered tours of their studios at Rockefeller Center. After the page greeted us with the network's famous three chimes, we walked around several studios, including *NBC Nightly News* and *Saturday Night Live*. The page was excited that *The Tonight Show* was moving to New York in 2014 and we were encouraged to return for a taping.

Since my 2014 trip was to see the Royals play at Fenway Park, I decided to pass through New York City on my way home. My sight-seeing time was limited, but I thought it would be special to attend a taping of *The Tonight Show Starring Jimmy Fallon*. Standby tickets are issued outside Rockefeller Center starting at 9 am, so I mistakenly thought I could beat the crowd by arriving at 8:15. Once the pages began issuing tickets, I realized that I was unlikely to get into *The Tonight Show*, so I decided to ask for a ticket to *Late Night with Seth*

Meyers. Even though I had never watched the show, I knew a television taping was an experience I could not have in Missouri.

Changing my plans proved to be a wise decision. That evening's show included actress Kate Hudson, who was promoting her new movie *Wish I Was Here*, and David Remnick, editor of *The New Yorker*. Following his monologue, Seth Meyers presented some of the embarrassing *Late Night* sponsors, such as Lead-Lined Diapers and the North Korea Board of Tourism.

In addition to the entertainment value of the program, I enjoyed watching the process of making television. The show is taped in real-time, meaning that commercial breaks in the studio last the same length as those for the home audience. During one of the breaks, we watched Meyers and Hudson film promos for four NBC affiliates. Meyers took questions from the audience during another break. Meanwhile, set pieces were moved around constantly, even at times while the show was filming. I became a fan of *Late Night* that day and have watched many of the episodes since then. On a future trip, I may still try to attend a taping of *The Tonight Show*.

Wristband worn by each audience member
at the taping of *Late Night with Seth Meyers.*

Looking back, it is easy to see why New York looked overwhelming, even though I had been to other large cities like Chicago and Toronto. Once I learned to navigate the subway system and discovered that many of the destinations are close to each other, I came to love the city. It may take a lifetime to discover all that New York has to offer and I know I want to further explore the city's entertainment scene.

CHAPTER 15

This Is Not My Grandfather's Mass Transit

||||||||||||||||||||||||||||||||||||||||||||||||||||||||||||||||||||||||||||||||||||||||||||||||||||||||||||||||||||||||||||||||||||||||||||||||||||||||||||||||

My maternal grandparents never owned a car after the 1940s. They relied on the St. Paul and Minneapolis bus service for decades. My grandfather Poppo had a photographic memory and even though he was blind for the last 20 years of his life, he knew the St. Paul bus routes well and passed that on to me. The 34 bus went to downtown St. Paul and to Midway Shopping Center. The 7 bus traveled all the way to Signal Hills Shopping Center. The 4 bus followed Snelling Avenue, the 5 to Como Park, and so on. One of my favorite activities with Poppo was to take the 16 bus to downtown Minneapolis along University Avenue. Poppo loved to talk about the history of the buildings that he could no longer see along University. We would eat lunch in the Woolworth's cafeteria in the IDS Center.

The present Twin Cities mass transit is not what Poppo knew. Bus routes have been renumbered, rerouted, and discontinued. A light-rail system now follows University Avenue between the two cities' downtowns. I cannot conceive relying on public transportation for daily activities, but I have taken advantage of mass transit systems both in the United States and Canada.

Even though I grew up only 300 miles from Chicago, my childhood travels completely avoided the Windy City. We ventured from

Winnipeg to Orlando, from New Orleans to Milwaukee, but my parents had no desire to drive in Chicago. I decided in 2007 that it was past time for me to take my first trip to the nation's third-largest city. The problem was that I had heard horror stories about nightmarish traffic and expensive downtown parking. My first Chicago trip had four destinations: Shedd Aquarium, the Field Museum, Macy's on State Street, and of course, Wrigley Field. I wanted to figure out how I could maximize my sightseeing without living in traffic jams or bankrupting myself with parking fees.

One of the best pieces of travel advice I was ever given came from a dated source—a Usenet group. I posed a question about how to best access mass transit and was told to use the Park & Ride station at Interstate 90 and Cumberland Avenue near O'Hare Airport. The suggestion was perfect. The Chicago Transit Authority (CTA) operates a parking garage at the Blue Line "L" Cumberland station and as of early 2016, riders could park up to 12 hours for only $5. The Blue Line connects O'Hare to the Loop, from where riders can transfer to other buses and trains. I have often bought a pass allowing unlimited bus and train rides, providing access to both baseball stadiums, the Museum Campus, the Museum of Science and Industry, Navy Pier, the Chicago Temple, and the stores of State Street.

I love to visit Chicago, but do not enjoy sitting in Chicago traffic. Each time I visit Chicago I choose a hotel in one of the suburbs near O'Hare such as Arlington Heights or Schaumburg. Schaumburg has the sprawling Woodfield Mall, an IKEA store, and one of my favorite Italian restaurants in Moretti's. In the eight years since my initial trip, I have returned to Chicago nine times because using CTA from the Cumberland station has been convenient.

New York is another city with outstanding public transportation. I chose a hotel in Queens for under $140/night including parking that was within walking distance of the 7 subway connecting Times Square to Citi Field. On my first trip to the Big Apple, I bought a week-long pass and once I realized that most of the places I wanted to visit were clustered in Manhattan, I freely transferred from subway line to subway line, occasionally using a city bus. I found the trip planner on their website tripplanner.mta.info to be especially helpful. Every New York attraction I visited was convenient to a subway line.

Ads on the New York City subway commemorated the 2013 All-Star Game at Citi Field. For Royals fans, Citi Field is better known as the site of Game 5 of the 2015 World Series.

Atlanta was another city with public transportation that spared me several trips down congested interstates. I chose a hotel in the northeast suburb of Doraville, several blocks from the Gold Line light-rail station. The Gold Line takes riders to all the attractions of downtown Atlanta, including the state capitol and World of Coca-Cola. From downtown I transferred to a bus to the Martin Luther King Jr. National Historic Site.

The fourth U. S. city in which I greatly appreciated mass transit was Boston. Known locally as the "T", subway lines run across metropolitan Boston. I found the Riverside Green line, located just off

Interstate 95, to be the most convenient. As in Chicago and New York, I bought a versatile pass that allowed for transfers to other subway lines serving Boston Common, Faneuil Hall, and Cambridge. Many fans take the "T" to Fenway Park with stops several blocks on either side of the historic stadium. I made one of my planning mistakes with this 2014 trip, choosing a hotel in suburban Billerica that was not convenient to the Riverside station.

My Canadian travels have also been enhanced by public transportation. When I watched the Royals play the Toronto Blue Jays in 2012, I redeemed points for a downtown hotel and in four days, I moved my car only to visit Niagara Falls. Only a block from my hotel, the subway line connected the former Maple Leaf Garden to the Rogers Centre, Ontario Parliament Building, Royal Ontario Museum, and shopping at Toronto Eaton Centre. I could have also taken heavy rail lines to suburban destinations. Using the subway for four baseball games saved me considerable parking expense, even though I had to walk several blocks from Union Station to the Rogers Centre.

One reason I quickly fell in love with Montreal on that same trip was the ease of commuting. My hotel offered a free 24-hour shuttle van to the airport, where I caught the 747 express bus. I bought a three-day pass for unlimited bus and subway rides and especially appreciated the 747 bus, which stops along René Lévesque Boulevard downtown. The Saint Laurent Avenue stop is at the entrance to Chinatown, where I tried roast duck for the first time. Pedestrians may walk from Chinatown down to the Old Montreal historic district with dining, shops, Montreal City Hall, and the Notre-Dame Basilica. I used the Green line of the Montreal Metro subway to visit the city's botanical garden and their impressive collection of bonsai trees. Given how many miles I drove the rest of the trip, I was glad to leave my car in the hotel parking lots in Toronto and Montreal.

The most recent city in which I discovered mass transit was Vancouver. To save money, I chose a hotel in Surrey that was located minutes from the Scott Road SkyTrain station. Parking at the station was $3 and the Expo Line connected Surrey to downtown Vancouver, all the way to the waterfront. From downtown I transferred to a 19 bus to Stanley Park to visit the Vancouver Aquarium.

I probably rode my first bus before the age of four months. For my grandparents, the St. Paul and Minneapolis buses were necessities. While I could have maneuvered around the largest cities of the United States and Canada by car, the different forms of public transportation have enabled me to see more of these cities without the headaches and costs of traffic and parking.

CHAPTER 16

Small Town America

Traveling from Missouri to Minnesota in the 1980s and 1990s, before Iowa four-laned many of their major highways, I came to appreciate the small towns of America. My family had our standard route through Hannibal, Cedar Rapids, Waterloo, and Rochester, but each year we tried to vary our route on either the northbound or southbound drive. Through the years, we drove through many towns in southern Minnesota, eastern Iowa, and northeast Missouri. When I drive long distances, I appreciate the convenience and speed of the interstate, but I enjoy the chance to travel the two-lane roads and visit small towns. My favorite towns stand out by showcasing their national origins or providing unique experiences such as a 75,000 square-foot "drugstore".

When my grandparents were living, my favorite routes home from St. Paul were through Pella, Iowa, about 40 miles southeast of Des Moines. Pella spotlights its Dutch heritage with a Tulip Time festival each spring and has a visitor center inside a windmill. Jaarsma Bakery, on the town square, is a must-stop for Dutch letters and apple bread. When I watched a former student play football at Truman State University in Kirksville, Missouri, I left home at 5 am so I could include a side trip to Jaarsma Bakery. A glockenspiel on the town square gives four performances daily. Pella has many restaurants, both local and chain.

The tourist information center is one of many Dutch sites in Pella.

In addition to Pella, Iowa has several towns that showcase the nationality of their founders. Elk Horn showcases its Danish heritage (see Chapter 20). Swedesburg spotlights Swedish heritage and is home to the Swedish-American Museum. The Norwegian-American Museum is located in Decorah.

My first trip to Michigan was to see the Royals play in Detroit in 2007 and shortly before I left town, *Midwest Living* printed a travel guide of the Wolverine State. I learned about Frankenmuth, and even though the town was 25 miles out of the way, I am glad I took the side trip. Frankenmuth is modeled after Bavarian towns and includes two must-visits. I timed my trip to Frankenmuth for a fried chicken dinner at Zehnder's and recommend eating in the Z Chef's Café downstairs for the same quality chicken at a lower price. Bronner's Christmas Wonderland is a full superstore of Christmas ornaments and other seasonal merchandise. As part of the store's emphasis on keeping "Christ" in Christmas, the grounds include a replica of the Austrian chapel where the carol *Silent Night* was first sung in 1818. Each Christmas Eve when singing *Silent Night*, my mind momentarily drifts over to Frankenmuth.

A drugstore put the town of Wall, South Dakota on the map. Located at the edge of the Badlands, in the 1930s Ted Hustead invited travelers to Wall Drug with numerous billboards promoting free ice water. The ice-water tradition continues as advertisements along Interstate 90 and other highways beckon motorists to Wall. The store has grown far beyond a small-town drugstore and sells merchandise ranging from books to Black Hills Gold to western clothing to pottery. Wall Drug has a large dining area where I ate my first bison hot dog; the doughnuts are also highly recommended. An animated T-Rex delights visitors. The front building even includes an art gallery and chapel.

I had new appreciation for Disney World's Main Street after visiting the town of Marceline, Missouri. Walt Disney lived in Marceline for about four years as a boy and wanted to build a theme park in northern Missouri, but died before his plans could come to fruition. The former train depot has been converted into the Disney Boyhood Museum. When I visited in 2007, the museum's curator knew Disney personally and referred to him simply as "Walt". The museum showcases artifacts from Disney's boyhood and return visits. Walking down Main Street USA of Marceline, visitors can see how the entrance into the Magic Kingdom was inspired by the north-central Missouri town.

Several presidents come from small towns. The Herbert Hoover Presidential Museum is located in West Branch, Iowa and the Dwight Eisenhower Museum is in Abilene, Kansas. Calvin Coolidge hails from Plymouth Crossing, Vermont. Ronald Reagan has several sites in Illinois—his birthplace in Tampico, boyhood home in Dixon, and small museum at his alma mater Eureka College.

Many more towns are waiting to be discovered by escaping the interstates and traveling down the backroads of America. My travel experiences have been enriched in these towns and others.

Ronald Reagan, 40th President of the United States,
was born in this building in Tampico, Illinois.

CHAPTER 17

The Stranger Side of the Road

Often when sharing the stories of my travels, people find the unusual attractions to be the most interesting. Millions of Americans have visited the Space Needle, the Alamo, Walt Disney World, and Times Square, but how many people can say they have seen the World's Largest Frying Pan or Salem Sue? When I am driving a long distance in a single day, I stop frequently to stretch my legs and stay refreshed. Many of the attractions in this chapter require only a five-minute stop, the perfect chance to take a quick break.

My aunt, uncle, and their 10-year-old grandson visited St. Louis for my sister's high school graduation in the 1990s. I was placed in charge of entertaining my relatives as my parents were busy with graduation activities. I enjoyed playing the role of "tour guide", especially since this was my cousin's first visit to St. Louis. One morning we visited the St. Louis Science Center and stopped at the Missouri Bakery on The Hill, the Italian neighborhood best known as the boyhood home of Yogi Berra and Joe Garagiola. Knowing that Illinois would be a new state for my cousin, I drove them across the Mississippi River and showed the soon-to-be fifth grader the World's Largest Catsup Bottle.

Located on Illinois Highway 159 in Collinsville, the World's Largest Catsup Bottle once served as a water tower and reminds drivers that Brooks once manufactured catsup in Collinsville. The bottle uses the spelling "catsup" rather than "ketchup" as that was the preferred spelling at the time of its construction. Preservationists rescued the water tower from destruction in the 1990s.

Many unusual tourist spots dot the former Route 66 across its run from Chicago to Los Angeles. I have not traveled the historic highway west of Oklahoma City, although I would like to venture that direction on a future trip as I still have yet to visit many of the western stadiums. The information center of Dwight, Illinois is located in a restored 1930s-era gas station. Springfield, Illinois was already on my radar because of the Abraham Lincoln Presidential Museum and state capitol, but Route 66 passes through town and the Cozy Dog Drive In displays many photographs of the historic highway.

Several years ago I attended a college baseball game at Missouri University of Science and Technology and had planned to stop for dinner at Missouri Hick BBQ just east of Cuba on the way home. I exited Interstate 44 sooner and found the World's Largest Rocking Chair west of Cuba. The town has many murals commemorating the history of Route 66, providing photograph opportunities before a great barbecue dinner. I have also visited the Blue Whale of Catoosa, located in a Tulsa suburb.

The Blue Whale in Catoosa, Oklahoma is one of many quirky roadside attractions on or near historic Route 66.

In addition to the catsup bottle in Illinois, many places claim to have the largest version of a familiar animal or object. One year we were driving to Minnesota and noticed a billboard on Interstate 380 in Iowa advertising the World's Largest Frying Pan. Sure enough, there was a giant frying pan in the town of Brandon, although in later years the attraction was "downgraded" to Iowa's Largest Frying Pan.

A stretch of Interstate 94 in North Dakota provides two large versions of familiar animals. Jamestown showcases the World's Largest Buffalo. Two hours west in New Salem, Salem Sue, the World's Largest Holstein Cow, looks over the highway. Not to be outdone by their neighbors to the west, Frazee, Minnesota is home to the World's Largest Turkey.

Returning to the bovine theme, Audubon, Iowa is home to Albert the Bull, commemorating the state's beef industry.

Fictional characters also stand tall along the roadways. Douglas, Wyoming is home to the World's Largest Jackalope. While in Douglas, I also enjoyed visiting the Pioneer Memorial Museum. A statue of the Jolly Green Giant towers over Interstate 90 in Blue Earth, Minnesota.

Many of my students know I enjoy traveling as my classroom is decorated with photos of landmarks and attractions. One day a student asked if I had visited the World's Largest Toilet. I was sure she was pulling my leg and that no such place existed. She convinced me to run a Google search and sure enough, there is a World's Largest Toilet in Columbus, Indiana.

Just as when I visited Hell, Michigan, I was embarrassed to mention the name of the attraction when I arrived in Columbus in 2014. The commode is housed at the Kidscommons Children's Museum, but people wanting to just see it do not have to pay admission. I walked in the museum and started to say something like, "I understand you have a large version of a plumbing fixture." The worker interrupted me, "Yes, the World's Largest Toilet is on the third floor." The commode is large enough for a person to fit in the bowl and instead of an actual flush, the "drain" leads to stairs to the lower level. To this day, the picture of me inside the commode bowl is one of the most popular things I have posted on Facebook.

Proof that there actually is the World's Largest Toilet.
The commode is located in Columbus, Indiana.

Not every city can claim a presidential library or a baseball sta-dium or a national historic site. I have remembered many small towns for their unusual claims to fame. The oddball landmarks provide pho-to opportunities and a way to remember the lesser-known communi-ties and the roads less traveled.

CHAPTER 18

Living Things, Past and Present

As a teacher and host of trivia night competitions, I have found it important to have a variety of interests. Students would become bored if all my word problems focused on baseball and St. Louis Cardinals fans would be especially irritated if I emphasized the Kansas City Royals. A good trivia night will offer questions from a wide range of topics; many times I will pick a state and base a category on that particular state. Living near St. Louis, I have been familiar with zoos since I was small, but in recent years, I have expanded my travel to include aquariums and natural history museums.

I live less than a half-hour from the St. Louis Zoo, considered to be among the best in the country. Although its free admission is one of its marketing points, this is not a "get what you pay for" situation. Beginning with a flight cage from the 1904 World's Fair, the zoo has continued to expand through the decades, most recently renovating its bear pits. Raja the elephant is a popular attraction; he is the father of four, most recently Priya in 2013. The elephants, cheetahs, and hyenas are part of the River's Edge exhibit. Other exhibits built in the last 20 years include the Monsanto Insectarium, Penguin and Puffin Coast, and Caribbean Cove.

While most of the zoo's attractions are free, visitors may enhance their St. Louis Zoo experience. The Zooline Railroad takes passengers quickly from one area of the zoo to another, placing riders close to the tiger display. Foxes, tree kangaroos, and river otters are among the animals showcased in the Children's Zoo. Other ticketed attractions include the Conservation Carousel, a 4-D motion simulator, sea lion show, and movie at The Living World.

Fargo, North Dakota is home to the Red River Zoo, one of the newest zoos in the United States. Although smaller than many zoos, the Red River Zoo is home to unique species such as red pandas and gray foxes.

Mutual of Omaha was a long-time sponsor of the television program *Wild Kingdom*, so it was no surprise that the Henry Doorly Zoo in Omaha is one of the nation's largest. The Desert Dome displays snakes, roadrunners, ocelots, and a bearded dragon. Underneath the dome Kingdoms of the Night showcase nocturnal animals like aardvarks and alligators. The Lied Jungle is an indoor rainforest. Other notable exhibits include the Cat Complex, Hubbard Gorilla Valley, and the Butterfly and Insect Pavilion. An African Grasslands region is under construction and scheduled for completion in 2017.

When planning my first trip to Chicago in 2007, I asked a number of people familiar with the city to recommend tourist attractions and the Shedd Aquarium was at or near the top of most lists. Having never visited a large aquarium before, I did not know what to expect, but soon learned why Shedd is popular. The dolphin show, staged in a room with a view of Lake Michigan, is alone worth the price of admission. Other popular exhibits include a replica Caribbean coral reef and Oceanarium. Since my visit, Shedd Aquarium has built a 4-D theater.

Two years later I visited the Audubon Aquarium of the Americas in New Orleans. The highlight of the visit was the opportunity to feel both a shark and stingray and come face-to-face with a living crab. Given its location near the confluence, marine life from the Mississippi River and Gulf of Mexico is spotlighted.

Aquariums offer a great deal of variety as each showcases underwater life from its particular region. The Vancouver Aquarium offers shows starring sharks and beluga whales. The 4-D show featured sea monsters whose fossils have been discovered in recent years. One exhibit displayed the variety of species found off the coast of British Columbia. Underground viewing areas in some exhibits allow visitors a complete glimpse of northern marine life. Galleries spotlight life from the Amazon and tropical regions and visitors might be surprised to see African penguins. By visiting three aquariums in vastly different geographic regions, I have seen many marine species. Having gone to aquariums near the Great Lakes, Gulf of Mexico, and in the Pacific Northwest, I would like a future trip to include an aquarium in the eastern United States.

The beluga show was among the highlights
of a trip to the Vancouver Aquarium.

The people who gave me advice about visiting Chicago also recommended the Field Museum of Natural History for my first Windy City vacation. Best known for the most complete *Tyrannosaurus rex* fossil Sue, the Field Museum provides a comprehensive view of living

creatures throughout history. Thousands of specimens of living creatures have been displayed for decades. The upstairs gallery walked
visitors through natural history, through each of the five mass extinc-
tions, and suggested events that may lead to the sixth mass extinction
in the future. When I visited the museum in 2007, the special exhibit
at the time told the life story of Charles Darwin. The Field Museum is
a research institution and visitors may watch and ask questions of the
scientists preparing fossils.

Sue, the *Tyrannosaurus rex,* stands out at Chicago's Field Museum.

Another impressive natural-history museum is the Royal Ontario
Museum (ROM) in downtown Toronto. While visitors will find dinosaur skeletons and animal specimens common to natural-history
museums, the World Cultures galleries distinguish the ROM from its
American counterparts. Beginning with the Stone Age, tools, artifacts,
and artwork from millenniums of human culture are displayed. One
gallery displays textiles and costumes, some pre-dating the time of

Christ. I had one disappointment. Despite its name, the museum did not give a discount for Royals fans!

As I drove to Seattle in the summer of 2015, one of my unexpected discoveries was the Museum of the Rockies (MOR) in Bozeman, Montana. I knew I had picked the right summer to visit the museum when the traveling exhibit, originating from the Field Museum, featured the history of chocolate and its forms through the years. The large collection of *Tyrannosaurus rex* fossils are prominently featured, as well as other dinosaur species, including a *Triceratops*. The museum includes a history of the peoples who called the Rockies home. Antique-car enthusiasts will enjoy seeing a Ford Model A and early Oldsmobile. Visitors to the museum may also touch a piece of a meteorite. Admission to the Taylor Planetarium is included with the museum entrance fee.

Species life throughout the history of the earth is far more diverse than I could have imagined. Dinosaurs have long fascinated me, but standing next to their skeletons has increased my wonder about these prehistoric creatures. Living in the middle of the United States, far from an ocean, sea, or gulf, aquariums have provided the opportunity to view creatures not found in Midwest waterways. Present-day zoos display animals in settings often resembling their natural habitat. I hope that future trips will include different zoos, particularly when I eventually travel to San Diego, aquariums, and natural history museums.

CHAPTER 19

Up, Up, and Away

A replica of the Wright Brother's bicycle shop is part of the Dayton
Aviation Heritage National Historical Park.

The last time I was on an airplane was to fly to St. Paul to visit my
grandparents in the spring of 1994. I remember my ears hurting for

hours after the flight and the return trip was delayed for de-icing. Of course, the real reason I do not enjoy flying is that I miss all the interesting places between home and the destination city. Even though I prefer the highways, I have enjoyed visiting many aviation and space travel sites and hope to visit Kitty Hawk in the future.

Any discussion of flight naturally begins with the Wright Brothers and even though they flew from North Carolina, they built their business in Dayton, Ohio. The Dayton Aviation National Historic Park consists of five sites, most notably one of the Wright Brothers bicycle shops. From the historic park, I drove to the National Museum of the United States Air Force, located at Wright-Patterson Air Force Base outside Dayton. Over 360 aircraft and missiles are displayed, including the plane on which Lyndon Johnson took the presidential oath of office following John Kennedy's assassination. One section of the museum is dedicated to aviation pioneers and military buffs will enjoy the large collection of Air Force clothing and uniforms.

Huntsville, Alabama, known for Space Camp, is home to the U. S. Space and Rocket Center. The Apollo 16 capsule is prominently displayed. Other exhibits include a Saturn V rocket and the *Pathfinder*, the prototype for what became the Space Shuttle. I visited the museum in 2010 and since my trip, bus tours of the Marshall Space Flight Center have been added. Movies are regularly shown at the 3D and IMAX theaters.

My 2010 trip continued through the Southeast where I spent a day at the Kennedy Space Center. One highlight was taking the Shuttle Launch Experience; lockers are provided as guests must empty their pockets before the simulation. Visitors can touch a piece of moon rock. Rockets and modules are displayed. A bus tour takes visitors to the Astronaut Hall of Fame and provides great views of the launching pads which, at the time of my visit, were still used for space shuttles. The tour in 2010 included watching the building of parts for the International Space Station. Since my visit, Kennedy Space Center permanently displayed Space Shuttle *Atlantis*.

One of the most famous quotes from space was, "Houston, we

have a problem." Houston has been associated with space travel ever since and an important part of my 2009 Texas trip was a visit to the Houston Space Center. One of the exhibits gives visitors a feel for what daily life is like on the International Space Station, including the answer to the oft-asked question of how do astronauts use the restroom in space. Two movie theaters show films throughout the day. Among the spacecraft displayed are the Mercury 9 and Gemini 5 capsules, along with the Apollo 17 command module.

Concord, New Hampshire was already on my 2014 New England stop list because of the capitol building, but the McAuliffe-Shepard Discovery Center is another place to visit. Named for two New Hampshire astronauts, the museum was built as a planetarium to honor Christa McAuliffe following her death when Space Shuttle *Challenger* exploded in 1986. A scale model of Mercury 7 on which Alan Shepard became the first American in space is on display.

One last aviation site is the Future of Flight Aviation Center in Mukilteo, Washington, north of Seattle. The center includes a tour of Boeing, in which visitors see airplanes, including the Dreamliner, under construction. The visitor gallery displays many aircraft through the years, with all aspects of airplanes, from engines to passenger seating, included. Part of a Pan Am Airways plane is featured for guests nostalgic for the long-defunct airline.

Although I doubt I will ever travel into space, I know that if I am to reach my goal of visiting all 50 state capitol buildings, I will be back in an airplane someday. I have developed new appreciation for the early aviators, as well as more than a half-century of astronauts.

CHAPTER **20**

Book It

Mark Twain's influence is felt throughout Hannibal.

The literary world has a few interesting sites. If I had an unlimited pot of money, I might build a candy factory as depicted in *Charlie and the Chocolate Factory* and hope my workers sang as well as the Oompa Loompas.

A name most associated worldwide with my native Missouri is Mark Twain. Twain put the northeast Missouri town of Hannibal on the map. Outside his boyhood home, you can see the fence that Tom Sawyer famously brought in "outside contractors" to whitewash. Two other buildings are homes of the people who inspired the characters Huckleberry Finn and Becky Thatcher. The Mark Twain Boyhood Museum includes a Norman Rockwell gallery. Cardiff Hill is home to a statue of Tom Sawyer and Becky Thatcher. The Mark Twain Memorial Bridge carries Interstate 72 across the Mississippi River toward Springfield, Illinois.

My 2014 New England trip was guaranteed to include Hartford for a visit to the Connecticut State Capitol. However, this lifelong Missourian was stunned to learn that Hartford is also home to *The Mark Twain Museum* (italics theirs). The Hannibal and Hartford sites complement each other well, while Twain's Hannibal childhood inspired several books, he did much of his writing in Hartford. A Lego statue of Twain greets visitors to the Hartford museum. Visitors can see a Ken Burns mini-documentary. One of the museum's most notable exhibits is one of Twain's typesetting machines.

The summer of 2009 included my first baseball game in the Royals Triple-A city of Omaha. As I was returning home through Iowa, billboards on Interstate 80 promoted Elk Horn, one of the state's many small town gems. Elk Horn takes pride in its Danish heritage and is home to the Museum of Danish America. Hans Christian Andersen Park in Elk Horn includes a statue honoring *The Little Mermaid*.

Iowa's other literary treasure is the Roseman Covered Bridge, associated with the book and movie *The Bridges of Madison County*. Roseman is one of six surviving covered bridges in the county. Maps to all the bridges are available in downtown Winterset, a town also famous as the birthplace of John Wayne. My trip to the Roseman Bridge is one I remember especially fondly as I was heading home from St. Paul after celebrating my grandmother's 100th birthday in 2006, a trip mentioned in Chapter 22.

Springfield, Massachusetts is best known for the Basketball Hall of

Fame, but is also home to the Dr. Seuss National Memorial Sculpture Garden. Dr. Seuss, born Theodor Geisel, grew up in Springfield and the sculptures are appropriately located behind the city library. One statue contains the entire text of *Oh, the Places You'll Go*. The Cat in the Hat, Yertle the Turtle, Sam I Am, and Horton the elephant are among the characters represented.

Visiting these literary sites added to my appreciation for the books they represent.

CHAPTER 21

Sunday Morning Tourist

On most of my vacations, I have only two activities with firm time schedules—the baseball games and church services. I enjoy visiting other churches when I travel, meeting people, and hearing different sermons. My denomination, the United Methodist Church, is a connectional church, so I feel comfortable joining an unfamiliar congregation for morning worship. Although my stories all take place in Methodist churches, members of any denomination can enjoy discovering new churches as they travel.

My 2009 trip included all the major cities of eastern Texas, and I was thankful that the Houston Astros played in an air-conditioned, retractable-roof stadium. The temperatures regularly climbed over 100° on the trip and when I drove to Dallas, my car even showed 122° after sitting outside Dealey Plaza for several hours. When I attended church in Irving, I immediately discovered one difference between Texas and Missouri churchgoers. Unlike their Midwest counterparts, many attenders at Plymouth Park United Methodist Church carried their Bibles into church. I decided that the worshippers in suburban Dallas had a clear understanding of the climate of hell and did not want to take any chances.

Most of the churches I attend on vacation receive few visitors from Missouri, but coincidence has happened. West End United Methodist Church in Nashville, Tennessee advertised the largest pipe organ in the state (five manuals), so the church was a natural stop on my 2011 trip to the Grand Ole Opry. That afternoon I posted on Facebook that I attended the church and my parents' minister responded that the first wedding she ever performed was at West End.

Two of the churches I have visited draw large numbers of tourists. Wesley Monumental United Methodist Church in Savannah is located close to the town's statue of Methodist founder John Wesley. Knowing that parking might be scarce, I arrived at the church about a half-hour before the 8:45 service. Several of us in the pews chatted and I found out the other people were visiting from New Jersey and Washington, DC. An usher commented that he was always able to tell the members from the visitors because the visitors were the ones who arrived on time.

John Wesley welcomes travelers to Savannah.

The Chicago Temple downtown also draws a number of tourists. The sanctuary is located on the ground level of an office tower near a

Blue Line station and two blocks from Macy's on State Street. Above the tower is the Sky Chapel which was dedicated in memory of drugstore founder Charles Walgreen. The altar in the chapel depicts Jesus praying over the city of Chicago. Tours of the chapel are offered after services and during the week.

If I am in Kansas City on a Sunday morning, I usually attend Old Mission United Methodist in Fairway, Kansas. Most years I attend Old Mission only once or twice, but I apparently made an impression at some point. When the Royals were still in their lengthy run of futility, the minister (now retired) greeted me with, "I remember you. You're the person who brings the Royals bad luck." Sadly, he may have been right.

During my 2012 weekend in Vermont, I attended church in St. Albans, just south of the Canadian border. The church was transitioning that week to their summer schedule, so I had wanted to make sure I arrived at the correct time. Several days prior I contacted the church over Facebook to double-check the service time. The person who responded never told me his name, but when I walked in the sanctuary, he said, "You must be John." Obviously, I was surprised to be greeted by name over 1000 miles from home. The service was three days before Independence Day, so that morning's postlude was the only organ rendition I have heard of Lee Greenwood's *God Bless the USA*.

The Internet has made finding churches of any denomination easy. Worshipping in beautiful sanctuaries with great organs has been one of my favorite parts of traveling.

CHAPTER 22

Random Stories

Travel would lose its luster if I was not making memories. There are several stories of my road trips that do not fit into other chapters of this book. I share these recollections chronologically.

The City Museum field trip of 2002

It should come as no surprise that I enjoy taking my students on field trips. The first time I visited the City Museum, an unusual attraction in downtown St. Louis, was with over 100 seventh-graders in May 2002. Housed in an abandoned factory, the City Museum includes vintage arcade and pinball games, outdoor climbing areas, the world's largest pair of underwear, and tunnels. Shortly before we were scheduled to board the buses, three students said, "Mr. Brocato, why don't you crawl through the tunnel under the first floor?" Unfamiliar with the tunnel, I thought they had a great suggestion.

Midway through the tunnel, there was a hump that I could not figure how to cross. I spent what seemed like an eternity trying to figure out how to pass through the rest of the tunnel. I finally escaped the tunnel, but as I walked toward the entry area, I broke into a cold sweat and felt dizzy. One of my colleagues panicked and called the paramedics. I remember breathing into a paper bag and a parent giving me a cup of ice water. The paramedics checked my blood pressure and pulse and I rejoined everybody else for the rest of the field trip.

In the years following the City Museum story has evolved as subsequent students have embellished the tale. I left the tunnel without help from anybody, particularly the "jaws of life". Even though I panicked inside the tunnel, I did not swear and most definitely did not wet my pants. As far as I know, I did not terrify any small children behind me in the tunnel. I did learn my lesson and will never enter that tunnel again. On subsequent City Museum field trips, I have encouraged students to bring quarters as we have competed in a number of pinball games and Ms. Pac-Man.

Mommo's 100th birthday

About a year before my grandmother's 100th birthday on October 20, 2006, I realized that I would have that day off school as the Friday fell immediately following two evenings of parent-teacher conferences. A trip to St. Paul over a three-day weekend required careful planning and of course, luck with the weather as the upper Midwest occasionally receives snow in the late part of October. So we never told Mommo I was driving to Minnesota on her birthday. I had even mailed a birthday card earlier that week. Mom and Dad had traveled to St. Paul several days earlier, aware of my intentions.

I left home before 6 am the morning of her birthday. During the day Mom and Dad had let Mommo know there was a birthday surprise that would arrive later. Even with the early start, I knew I would not reach St. Paul until the late afternoon, especially with Friday rush hour traffic. When I arrived at her nursing home around 4:30 pm, Mom and Dad informed me that I might have to compete with a dog who delivered flowers earlier in the day. Despite my canine "rival", Mommo was thrilled that I drove more than 500 miles to celebrate her birthday with her. The next afternoon my parents and I threw a party at the nursing home. After the party I shared some pictures of my summer travels and my students before I drove that evening to Des Moines to make the Sunday drive more manageable.

Unfortunately, that trip would be the last time I saw Mommo as she passed away shortly before Christmas. Looking back, I am amazed that I was able to pull off an 1100-mile round trip over a three-day weekend and when Mom and Dad returned to Missouri a few days after me, they said how much it meant to Mommo that I was able to come even for a brief visit.

As I drove Interstate 35 through northern Iowa the evening of October 21, I rediscovered the Grand Ole Opry. Although I had grown up listening to the Opry on clear-channel radio, I had not heard a broadcast in years and that weekend the show was celebrating its anniversary. Since then I have often listened to the Opry when driving on Friday or Saturday evening and as I mentioned earlier, Dad and I attended a performance in 2011.

Where was I when Michael Jackson died?

In 2009 I attended an interleague series between the Royals and Houston Astros at Minute Maid Park. The final game of the series was on Thursday afternoon and I drove to San Antonio following the game. As I often do when attending Royals games, I listened to the post-game show on the radio. The host of the following program promoted that his guest would be the chair of the Texas House of Representatives Education Committee. I decided to keep the radio on and learn about another state's education issues.

During the interview, the network broke with an update first that Michael Jackson was taken to the hospital and later that he had died. Just as people alive in the 1960s remember where they were when they learned that President John Kennedy had been shot, whenever I see or hear the question asking where people were when Michael Jackson died, I reply with, "Interstate 10 somewhere between Houston and San Antonio".

Disney World at the best possible price

In Chapter 2, I shared the ways I have stretched my travel budget through the years. My best travel bargain was the price I paid for a one-day pass to the Magic Kingdom in 2010—zero dollars and zero cents. When I checked into my hotel in Lake Buena Vista, Florida, I noticed a kiosk offering discounted tickets to Orlando-area attractions, including Walt Disney World. I walked over to the booth and the person offered me a free ticket. The catch was that I would have to attend a presentation the next morning on a time-share vacation home.

Since I seldom visit Florida, I knew that nobody could persuade me to join a time-share program. Of course I could not admit during the presentation that I had come only for the free Disney World ticket. The presentation was interesting until the high-pressure sales began. I met with several sales agents, telling each one that I could not purchase property at that time. Although I did not enjoy the pressure, I reminded myself that I was saving $84. The presentation ended at 10 am and I enjoyed a free day at the Magic Kingdom, paying only for parking and meals.

Conquering the New Jersey Lottery

My favorite New Jersey souvenir was not purchased at Carlo's Bake Shop. I did not even bring home the best thing I bought in the Garden State. In 2014 I was driving from New York City to Pittsburgh to catch a Pirates/Dodgers game on my return home. I stopped at Carlo's Bake Shop and decided to take a southern route to Interstate 80 in order to pass through different towns. At a 7-Eleven store in Washington, I bought a $1 New Jersey Lottery instant ticket. The ticket offered five chances to match the numbers 1 or 14.

The first scratch revealed a 14, winning a $5 prize. Already considering this ticket a successful purchase, I next uncovered a "5X" symbol, quintupling that chance's $5 prize to $25. Thirty dollars was more than I had ever won on an instant lottery ticket, but my luck continued, matching a 1 for another $10. Neither of the last two numbers produced winners, but the $40 total prize paid for my ticket to that evening's Pirates game.

As delicious as Carlo's Bakery goods are,
this was the best thing the author ever purchased in New Jersey.

Driving the gauntlet

Returning from the Pacific Northwest in 2015, I knew that driving from Tacoma to Omaha in three days would prove taxing. I wanted to attend an Omaha Storm Chasers baseball game on the third day and a Kansas City Royals game the next day, so I accepted the "gauntlet". The first day consisted of a 700-mile drive from Tacoma to Bozeman, Montana.

I thought the second day of my drive would be the "easy" day as I would quickly stop at Old Faithful and then drive to Laramie, Wyoming. My idea had two flaws. First, I learned that Yellowstone National Park consists of many more attractions than just a single geyser. Second, I greatly underestimated the size of Wyoming.

Several weeks before my trip I received an e-mail promoting the Grand Prismatic Spring as a must-visit attraction. I figured that I had plenty of time to visit two attractions within Yellowstone. But as I drove through the national park, I kept discovering places to stop—the 45th parallel, Tower Falls, Gibbon Falls, Grand Fountain Geyser, and the Yellowstone Visitor Center. If I had not started to worry about time, I probably would have stopped at more attractions.

My time problem began after leaving Old Faithful when I saw a sign that the city of Cody was still 100 miles away. I ended up eating lunch at Bubba's Bar-B-Que in Cody at nearly 5 pm. Knowing that I still had to drive to Laramie, I was scared to look at the map because I did not want to see that Laramie was 250 miles away. I decided I had better check the atlas anyway and was stunned to learn I still had 383 miles left to drive. After a few not-particularly-Methodist words crossed my mind, I had to choose between pouting or making forward progress toward Laramie. Of course I started driving and arrived in Laramie four minutes before midnight. I enjoyed the beauty of Yellowstone and would not have changed a thing, except perhaps choosing a hotel closer to Cody.

Luckily the next day's drive was entirely on Interstate 80. The three-day gauntlet ended in Omaha that afternoon. I saw the Storm Chasers win that evening and the Royals win the next day in Kansas City, so the story has a happy ending. I have learned to allow more time in the future when visiting national parks.

A well-planned vacation should offer many chances to make great memories. Some of those moments, though, cannot be predicted, yet they turn into wonderful stories.

CHAPTER **23**

What Comes Next?

So far I have visited 41 states and four Canadian provinces. Except for the Pacific Northwest, I have not yet traveled to most of the western states. East of the Mississippi, I have yet to enter Virginia or the District of Columbia, surprising many people who know my vacations and especially my interest in government and historical sites.

After visiting Safeco Field in the summer of 2015, I have attended games in 21 of the 30 MLB stadiums. Five of the remaining nine stadiums are in California. The other ballparks I have yet to visit are in Washington, Phoenix, Miami, and Milwaukee, although when I was in high school, we saw the Royals play at the old Milwaukee County Stadium—the first time I ever attended an MLB game played on natural grass as both Missouri ballparks had Astroturf until the mid-1990s. The Atlanta Braves are replacing Turner Field with a suburban ballpark in 2017, so the new stadium will immediately join my "must see" list. Atlanta will likely be the first city in which I attend games in three stadiums as we went to the old Fulton County Stadium on our way to Walt Disney World in 1990.

Minor-league baseball offers many opportunities to visit different cities and meet new mascots. I have attended games in only 10 of the 30 current Triple-A ballparks, many of which are located in major cities. Near the top of my list would be the new First Tennessee Park in Nashville, continuing the city's country music association with a guitar-shaped video board.

As an aside, many baseball fans have a hard time telling the two Triple-A leagues apart. My answer is that all the teams in the International League play their home games in the United States while the Pacific Coast League includes teams in Memphis and Nashville.

Once the Huntsville Stars moved to Biloxi in 2015, I could no longer say I had attended a game in any current Double-A city. My first priority would be to watch the Royals affiliate play in Springdale, Arkansas, one of the few Kansas City affiliates I have yet to see in person. The Royals also have lower affiliates in Lexington, Kentucky and Burlington, North Carolina that I have not watched.

With the exception of Maryland in 2008, I have been able to visit the capitol each time I have added a state. The only southeastern capitol I have yet to tour is in Montgomery, Alabama, but that should be easy to accomplish when visiting the newer baseball stadiums in Miami and Atlanta. At some point I envision taking a trip that includes Annapolis, Richmond, and Washington.

California might require a stay of several weeks. In addition to all the major and minor league ballparks, the state has two presidential libraries (Richard Nixon and Ronald Reagan). I probably would want to drive through Yosemite National Park, budgeting more time than I allowed for Yellowstone. I have heard all my life that the San Diego Zoo is a must-visit. Having watched the show for decades, I might even look into attending a taping of *The Price Is Right*. Knowing the electric atmosphere of *Late Night with Seth Meyers*, I cannot even begin to conceive the studio experience when audience members have the chance to win thousands of dollars in cash and prizes. My dad lived in San Leandro in the late 1960s and he has encouraged me to visit San Francisco.

I would like to visit all the provinces of Canada. Perhaps my next trip to New England will include a drive through the Maritime Provinces. Since I toured Vancouver in 2015, I would like to try planning the ferry trip to Victoria the next time I visit the Pacific Northwest. Thirty years have passed since I was in Winnipeg and I have never entered Alberta or Saskatchewan.

Given my family's history of living near the Mississippi River and my many trips to Minnesota, one bucket list item will surprise people. I have never viewed the headwaters of the Mississippi River at Lake Itasca. I envision a future trip through northern Minnesota, driving through Brainerd and Bemidji, and repeating my family's 1991 drive along Lake Superior's north shore from Duluth to Thunder Bay. One memory of that drive was stopping at Betty's Pies in Two Harbors, a restaurant that has since relocated, but I am sure the pie is as good as I remember. I once suggested to my grandparents that instead of the Land of 10,000 Lakes, Minnesota could be called the Land of 10,000 Desserts! Speaking of pie and the Upper Midwest, several people have remarked that I need to repeat our 1988 drive across Interstate 94 in Wisconsin and return to the Norske Nook in Osseo.

The list of destinations within the United States is unlimited. As I planned my 2015 trip west, many people offered suggestions of "must visit" locations. In addition to Victoria, time constraints kept three other suggested places off my itinerary. I would like to drive through the Grand Tetons and Jackson Hole, and will do so on a future trip, but looking back, I cannot even imagine how late I would have arrived in Laramie that evening. Glacier National Park sounded beautiful, but would have been 100 miles out of the way when I had planned a baseball game in Idaho Falls. Finally, a former colleague recommended Pioneer Village in Minden, Nebraska, but that fell at the end of the "Tacoma to Omaha gauntlet" and I had already planned the Archway Museum and an Omaha Storm Chasers game that day.

Spring training is one baseball experience that I lack and will probably have to wait until after I retire. The Royals train in the Phoenix suburb of Surprise and would require a 2-3 day drive each way with minimal stopping—not my favorite way to travel! I know people who have attended spring-training games in either Arizona or Florida and they have raved about the small ballparks and opportunities to interact with the players.

I have yet to hear about many of the places I will visit in the future.

Once I have selected a destination, I will discover lesser-known attractions in the city or along the way. Some of my favorite stops have been planned that day or even last minute after reading a highway sign or billboard.

Finally, I should mention that I would like to travel overseas once I have achieved my goals of visiting all 30 major-league baseball stadiums and 50 state capitol buildings. My trip abroad would likely include visiting the historic Methodist sites in England. I studied Spanish for four years in high school and even though my language skills do not resemble fluency, I have wanted to visit Spain since my freshman year. Family heritage travel would take me to Italy and Scandinavia.

I hope that this book has inspired you to travel across the United States and Canada. Discover the beauty, history, and ingenuity that are hallmarks of our great land. Of course, if you attend a Kansas City Royals baseball game, please bring home a winner!

Epilogue—Celebrating Royally

When the Royals won the 1985 World Series, I was in seventh grade. In the days following the Royals win over the local St. Louis Cardinals, I apparently became too big for my britches, according to people who knew me then. I gloated too much in the following days, with one of my teachers even threatening to give me a swirly. My 12-year-old mind assumed that the Royals would win many more titles in the coming years, probably as soon as 1986.

The Royals, of course, did not win the World Series in 1986, or even contend for a playoff spot. Despite a second Cy Young season from Bret Saberhagen, a third batting title for George Brett, and Bo Jackson's exploits, the Royals did not advance to the playoffs in the following seasons, either. For years, the Royals best stretch of baseball was a 14-game winning streak in 1994, weeks before a strike wiped out the remainder of the season and playoffs. Following the strike, the Royals slashed payroll and descended to the bottom of the standings, with one reminder of past glory being an episode of *The Simpsons* in which the family visited a book outlet store and blew dust off a tome titled, *Kansas City Royals: Forever Champions.*

As losses and empty stadium seats piled up, I tried to maintain a sense of humor about the situation. I reminded people that one of the perks of being a Royals fan was never needing to buy advance tickets! Maybe the highlight of attending a 10-0 afternoon loss would be stopping for pizza at Shakespeare's on the drive home. (Admittedly, the 2004 rain-delayed doubleheader sweep by the Montreal Expos still has no redeeming qualities, except for maybe how quickly I was able to exit the parking lot.)

A few years ago my friend Ryan and I were watching the Minnesota Twins play the Texas Rangers at the Metrodome on a night when the home team was struggling. After the Twins pitcher plunked a batter, one fan behind me said, "Is there anything else that can go wrong"? I turned around and responded, "I am from Missouri. My favorite team is the Kansas City Royals. You really do not want to know the answer to that question." Assuming I was joking, the fans laughed, but soon realized I was serious minutes later when Gary Matthews Jr. belted a grand slam as the Twins ended up losing 9-0.

Many people who were not alive in the 1980s did not understand how I could be a Royals fan. To them, the Royals were fodder for late-night monologues, not a franchise that once had a proud history. Stories about their comebacks in the 1985 postseason or meeting Frank White at a 1987 signing at the long-defunct Bannister Mall or watching Kevin Seitzer deliver six hits in a game seemed like ancient history. Meanwhile, the Cardinals were giving their fans season after season of excitement, whether it was Mark McGwire's record-setting home run totals or winning division titles, pennants, and the 2006 and 2011 World Series.

This is not to say there were no good times. I had the chance in 2003 to watch my high-school classmate Morgan Burkhart pinch-hit for the Royals in a game at Busch Stadium, a contest later punctuated by a game-ending third strike to Albert Pujols. A highlight of my 2009 trip to Houston was chatting with then-manager Trey Hillman before a ballgame and three years later I struck up a conversation with pitcher Bruce Chen before a game in Toronto. I learned to cherish every Royals win, even when it meant remaining at the stadium until 3:14 am.

Following the Royals acquisitions of James Shields and Wade Davis, the team started to win more frequently. Winning streaks lasted longer and double-digit losing streaks moved further into the past. Yet I continued to have unfortunate luck watching the Royals play, such as wasting Shields' brilliant pitching in a 1-0 Opening Day loss in Chicago in 2013 or a Red Sox sweep spoiling my first trip to Fenway Park in 2014.

Despite the Royals ending a 29-year playoff drought and advancing to the World Series in 2014, the end of the season felt unsatisfying. The Royals stranded the tying run on third base in the bottom of the ninth inning of Game 7 and despite the near-miss, I was still frequently hearing middle-school students repeat the phrase "Royals suck". The one difference was that I could respond, "That's American League champion Royals to you."

As mentioned in Chapter 11, I attended the Royals 10-1 Opening Day win over the Chicago White Sox. This was the third time I had gone to a Royals home opener, yet the first time the Royals had won the game. After the team improved to 7-0 a week later, I began to think that maybe the Royals players saw last season as unfinished business and that 2015 had the chance to turn into something special. Still, the Royals decades-long futility reinforced skepticism in my mind, why this life-long Missourian believes strongly in the statement, "I'm from Missouri. You have to show me."

I did not have the chance to attend another game until the last week in May, when the Royals played a series at Wrigley Field, their first in years. I bought an advance ticket for the opener on Friday and spent the morning walking and early afternoon walking around the Loop. True to my travel experiences, I encountered a soaking downpour when I stepped outside Macy's on State Street. At the same time, I saw another person wearing a Royals jersey and I remarked to him that I was glad I would not be alone. Several other Royals fans were riding the Red Line to Wrigley with me.

As it turned out, there were thousands of Royals fans who had traveled to the Cubs historic stadium. Throughout the game, I heard chants of "Let's Go Royals" in the stadium. Despite surrendering a four-run lead, the Royals pulled out the 8-4 win on the windy (but fortunately by then, dry) Chicago afternoon. Following the game, I walked to Byron's Hot Dogs on Irving Park Road, a hole-in-the-wall

Chicago institution featured in *GQ* magazine and once visited by President Barack Obama. Many Royals fans, including some who had not attended the game, were walking along Sheffield Avenue or sitting at the outdoor bars, high-fiving other Royals fans. I would not have seen this ten years earlier when the Royals were losing 100 games.

The winning improved attendance at Kauffman Stadium—not just on Opening Day. Lorenzo Cain Bobblehead Day required arriving nearly three hours ahead of first pitch just to be among the first 15,000 fans. Even a Thursday afternoon game with the Rays drew over 32,000 fans, double or triple what a similar game would have drawn during the losing seasons. I had to change my habits to begin buying tickets in advance. I also learned that leaving the parking lot would now take time—no longer could I count on entering Interstate 70 ten minutes after the last out nor arriving at Shakespeare's Pizza by 6 pm following an afternoon game.

I was most astounded by the support of Royals fans when I attended the June series in Seattle. Given the distance from Kansas City to Seattle and knowing that not many people have a burning desire to drive hundreds of miles across sparsely-populated regions of Montana and Idaho, I expected to be one of few Royals fans at Safeco Field. Not having great hope for the series opener with Felix Hernandez starting for the Mariners, I bought a ticket in the upper deck and much to my surprise, I heard familiar chants of "Let's Go Royals" and "MOOOOOOOOSE" in the stadium. A large group of Royals fans bought tickets behind the visiting dugout and their support could be heard in the upper level as the Royals defeated King Felix 4-2.

The next day at the Space Needle, I chatted with a number of Royals fans, some of whom had attended the game the night before and others who were just arriving in town. I had already decided to buy field-level tickets for the remaining two games and sitting among hundreds of blue-clad faithful far from Kauffman Stadium added to my Seattle experience. After suffering a shutout loss in the second game, the Royals won the rubber game on Wednesday and of course, there were more high-fives and handshakes with other fans.

Another part of the Royals fan experience in 2015 was remaining at the stadium following wins, both home and away. When the Royals win at Kauffman Stadium, the postgame player interviews are broadcast on the large center-field video board and usually the heroic player receives a bath from the dugout water bucket. Following the win in the third game in Seattle, the fans behind the dugout remained and watched the Fox Sports interviews as they were telecast back to the Midwest.

After not attending any postseason games in 2014, I decided that I would make every effort to attend my first playoff game at Kauffman Stadium in October 2015. My long-time friend from college Scott and I decided that we would attend the Division Series opener with the Astros. Scott and I have attended many Royals games through the years and he was the person who texted that he had seen me on TV during the 2013 rain delay in St. Louis at 1:30 am. Unfortunately, the Royals struggled offensively, except for two Kendrys Morales home runs, as Houston took the opener 5-2. Even though the Royals lost, attending a playoff game in Kansas City crossed an item off my bucket list, although not surprisingly given my travel habits, that bucket was filling with the rain that delayed the game in the third inning.

Having experienced decades of futility, like most Royals fans, I am conditioned to expect the worst. When the Royals were six outs from elimination by the Astros and trailing by four runs, despair set in and I absolutely was not taking any phone calls from relatives in the Houston area. Of course, the Royals rallied with seven runs in the eighth and ninth innings as the phrase "keep the line moving" was introduced to the fanbase. After Johnny Cueto dominated in the decisive Game 5, I started to think that maybe this could be a team of destiny.

Having a friend in Kansas City proved beneficial throughout the playoffs. Scott texted me with regular updates while I was attending a college football game and the Royals were overcoming a three-run deficit to defeat Toronto. Fast forward to Game 5 of the World Series and he and I exchanged many texts during the Royals ninth-inning

ROAD TRIPS, ROUTES, AND ROYALS

comeback and ultimate twelfth-inning clinching win. I felt like we were sharing the championship moment together despite watching the game some 250 miles apart.

Two days later came another bucket list item—the World Series parade. I left early and listened to AM 610, the Royals flagship radio station, from Kingdom City to Kansas City. I thought I would have time to shop for championship gear before the parade, but hearing how traffic was building downtown and parking lots were filling, I allowed only enough stopping time to use the restroom, buy a newspaper, and pick up snacks at Hy-Vee. By the time I arrived at the remote shuttle parking lot at Kemper Arena, the line for the shuttle was so long that I decided to walk to the parade.

Some estimates had 800,000 people attending the World Series parade. Even with my math background, I did not attempt a count, but there were sidewalks in which even walking was nearly impossible due to the crowds. Watching the players and coaches ride down Grand Avenue one-by-one brought back memories of the 15 games I had attended in 2015, from Seattle to St. Louis, from Opening Day to Game 1 of the American League Division Series. Manager Ned Yost with the World Series trophy was as awaited as Santa's arrival at the Macy's Thanksgiving Parade. I walked toward the post-parade pep rally at Union Station, but soon learned that was not possible due to the crowd. As it turned out, I knew several other people attending the parade, but trying to find them would have been like searching for a needle in a haystack. I enjoyed listening to the rally highlights on the radio following one last 2015 barbecue meal at Winslow's.

Several weeks later I watched the MLB Network telecast of the parade on my DVR. One of the announcers even remarked about the fan support, even at road games, and specifically mentioned the turnout for the series in Seattle. Later on I listened to a replay of the Royals broadcast of Game 5 of the World Series and moments before the clinching out, announcer Ryan Lefebvre talked about the loyalty of the fans throughout 2015. I felt that I was part of something special. Tens of thousands of miles traveled from Seattle to Atlanta, from

Houston to Boston, to watch the Royals play through the years finally paid dividends with the parade a perfect reason to take an unusual November trip to Kansas City.

The Promised Land is reached! Royals manager Ned Yost and the 2015 World Series trophy ride down Grand Boulevard in the November 3 parade.

CPSIA information can be obtained
at www.ICGtesting.com
Printed in the USA
FSOW04n2159281116
27896FS